CW00504374

"Parenting is one of those extremely impo[rtant] a trial run. But by its very nature paren[ting] the best they can do is to get the whole [...] *Big Picture Parents* is extremely useful f[or] that will position parents in the best plac[e ...] [...] children. It is to be highly commended."

—**Michael Hill**, former vice-principal and lecturer in Ethics, Moore Theological
   College, Sydney; author of *The Heart of Marriage* and *The How and Why of Love*

"A timely book for today's culture, *Big Picture Parents* is a lifeline for parents drowning in information overload. In a society that constantly twists the values, roles, and priorities of parents, Harriet Connor guides our feet to the solid ground of God's Word. She masterfully uses Scripture to lay an unshakable foundation for building an eternal parenting philosophy. If your head is spinning in self-doubt, take a step back and let this valuable resource renew your perspective."

—**Sara Wallace**, author of *The Gospel-Centered Mom*

"*Big Picture Parents* is a welcome addition to the pantheon of parenting wisdom. Rather than taking us down the 'practical' burrow, Harriet Connor lifts our eyes to the big picture of parenting: what God's purposes are for people, parents, and families, and how that picture ought to shape our parenting convictions and practices. I am an unashamedly 'big picture' person and this book warmed my heart!"

—**Lesley Ramsay**, Bible teacher, author of *A Taste for Life*; co-author of
   What Women Really Need

"Harriet Connor writes with refreshing honesty about some of the anxieties and frustrations of modern parenting. *Big Picture Parents* is sprinkled with helpful, true-life anecdotes to illustrate key points. As well as writing about the meaning of unconditional love for children and the limits of parenting, she writes wisely about a parent's key role: this is not to just steer children towards physical maturity but to also guide them towards moral maturity."

—**Kim Oates** OAM, pediatrician, emeritus professor, Sydney University Medical School; author of *20 Tips for Parents—The Realistic Parent's Guide to Understanding and Shaping your Child's Behaviour*

"What I really like about Harriet Connor's *Big Picture Parents* is that she takes you to the Bible to see God's plan for men and women living in a world broken by sin. We read of the struggles and challenges God's people face as they seek to live for him, we learn how to care for our families without guilt or fear, and we learn how to pass on the knowledge of God in many ways."

—**Christine Jensen** OAM, former president of Mothers' Union, Sydney; mentor to women in the Anglican Diocese of Sydney, Australia

Dedicated to my grandmothers—
to Elizabeth Anne Lorrimer, for inspiring me as a mother;
and to Amy Gladys McGrath, for inspiring me to write.

Contents

entire nation of parents agree on how to raise children? But by and large, throughout France they do. By contrast, in our society, there seem to be so many different ways of parenting. Most young parents I know are confused and uncertain about what to do.

Part of the reason for this is that our generation is much more mobile and multicultural than that of our parents and grandparents. We are more likely to move away from where we grew up, or to marry someone from a different cultural tradition. Because of this, we are not so firmly grounded in a single, local community, bound together by a common set of values. In the past, the adults in a community generally agreed on the attitudes and behaviors that were acceptable. Even the local bus driver or shop keeper had tacit permission to "parent" other people's children when they were not around. But no one would dare to do that today! Raising children is now seen as a private affair, with each family determining their own attitudes and values. This can make us feel like there are a thousand different ways to raise a child, and it is up to us to work out our approach from scratch.

But for most of human history, parenthood was a skill gained in the way an apprentice learns a trade. First, you watched an experienced practitioner (a "master"); then you assisted with the work, gaining the necessary skills along the way; and finally, you qualified as a practitioner in your own right.

My grandmother talks about how she had the chance to practice looking after a baby from the age of fourteen; her older sister had moved home to have her first child, because her husband was away fighting in the Second World War. The "master" parent of the house was my great-grandmother. She was permanently confined to a wheelchair due to rheumatoid arthritis. But while she and her husband were happy (and able) to employ staff to help with the cooking and cleaning, they felt that raising children was something they could never delegate. And so, my grandmother and her sister watched and learnt from my great-grandmother. Within the apprenticeship model, one person simply passes on the values, attitudes and skills that were passed onto them.

By contrast, I am a "childcare kid." From a very young age I did not see my parents or my sister during business hours. I had never seen a stay-at-home mother in action until I became one! Many of my mother's generation relied on their mothers and mothers-in-law to mind their children while they went out to work. But the working mothers of the eighties have become the working grandmothers of today. Consequently, many of them are not around during the week to offer hands-on help and advice to their adult children. And so, a lot of wisdom about parenting is being lost between the generations. When we "outsource" childminding to professionals outside the family, our collective wisdom can become fractured. As we watch paid experts relate to our children, we can also begin to feel that we do not have the necessary qualifications to raise our own children.

In the absence of "master parents" to learn from, our generation usually turns to our peers or, more commonly, to the internet for guidance. But there we find that the field of parenting has become a battlefield, staked out by experts with strong and conflicting opinions about how parents *should* be doing things, backed up by (apparently) scientific studies proving that any other way is harming your children. An apprenticeship is no longer enough—it seems that now you need a university degree even to qualify as a parent. In fact, I have a friend who, for that very reason, undertook a diploma of childcare when she became a mother.

Parenting in our generation feels harder than ever before, because we are completely overloaded with information about what we should be providing for our children. In the past, parents did not know so much about the science of their parenting; they just did their best with the information they had, gaining confidence through experience and observation. Apart from the occasional rebel, most people did more or less what their parents had done before them.

But in our generation, we have access to reams of scientific information about what our children should eat, how much they should sleep, what emotional needs they have at each stage, how they should play, what educational opportunities they need, and so on. This greater access to information has no doubt improved life for children in many ways. But there is a catch—the more access we have to information and resources, the more responsible we feel to provide the best for our children. The more we know about what we *should* be giving our children, the greater guilt we feel about falling short.

It feels like there is a parenting expert whispering in my ear all day, and it makes me feel guilty: "Have they had their five servings of vegetables today? Shouldn't they sleep for a bit longer? Have they practiced some age-appropriate gross and fine motor skills this week? Did you check how much sugar was in that snack? Aren't they watching too much TV?"

But all of this information and advice crowds out the more important questions of parenthood. We are so caught up on the tiny details—all the "shoulds and shouldn'ts"—that we forget to step back and ask ourselves what parenthood is all about. We might be able to tell you our views on bottle feeding, co-sleeping, smacking (spanking), screen time, sugar, childcare, and so on. But very few of us can tell you exactly what we are aiming for, or how we plan to get there. We have lost sight of the bigger picture.

As a result, many of us are struggling to make sense of our lives. We know how to make ourselves happy for a moment, but not for a lifetime. We have created many "small pictures" to give our life meaning—our job, our interests, our house, our children, our holidays, our causes—but we have a sneaking suspicion that perhaps they don't add up to much.

The loss of a big picture is certainly having an impact on modern parents. Jennifer Senior, author of *All Joy and No Fun: the Paradox of Modern Parenthood* writes,

> There's no denying that our lives as mothers and fathers have grown much more complex, and we still don't have a new set of scripts to guide us through them. Normlessness is a very tricky thing. It almost guarantees some level of personal and cultural distress.[2]

In her book, *Toxic Childhood: How the Modern World is Damaging Our Children and What We Can Do About It*, Sue Palmer writes,

> Most parents are frantically doing their best in a world where the goal posts are not just moving—they've actually disappeared . . . In a world of tumultuous change, confidence is thin on the ground. The moral and social certainties that once produced the adult alliance have disintegrated, and there seems to be nothing to put in their place.[3]

Reconnecting with Wisdom from the Past

A lifeline for me has been talking to my grandmothers on the phone. They can remember what it was like to be at home with small children, and a chat with them always helps to put things into perspective. It helps me to sift out the momentary fads of our time from the time-tested wisdom of generations. I often ask find myself asking, "What would Granny have done?"

2. Senior, *All Joy and No Fun*, 7.
3. Palmer, *Toxic Childhood*, chapter 10, para. 4; chapter 10, section 2, para. 1.

It might sound strange, but I have always had a deep desire to live a life that would make my ancestors proud. They lived through times that were much tougher than ours, often characterized by war, disease, and poverty. Daily life was plain hard work, with little choice and little comfort. I often find myself telling our boys how their great-grandparents, who were children during the Great Depression, would have been excited just to get an orange in their Christmas stocking!

In the West, our lives are so different now—brimming with choice and comfort. One of my great-grandmothers was still alive when I was younger—she was born in 1900, and lived to the age of ninety-seven. In her lifetime alone, she witnessed incredible changes. When my great-grandmother was born, only the rich had a telephone or a car, and the arrival of television was still half a century away!

I don't want our modern comforts to turn me or my children into the "spoiled brats" down the bottom of the family tree. I don't want to get swept along by the currents of our era and lose touch with the big values that got my ancestors through the toughest of times. And so I love to listen to my grandmothers talk about what life was like in previous generations.

As I have listened carefully to the wisdom of my grandmothers, I have realized that there is more to their advice than just scattered bits of useful information. Their wisdom is embedded in a much bigger picture—a whole way of thinking about the world. Their generation inherited this way of thinking from their parents, who inherited it from their parents before them, and so on. And in the West, that worldview—that "big picture" in which they parented—had grown out of Christianity.

Beginning with the conversion of the Roman Emperor Constantine in the fourth century, the Christian view of the world gradually won over the hearts and minds of the people of Europe. And it was this worldview, taught in the pages of the Bible, which shaped European cultural ideas about the meaning of life and consequently, parenthood.

One of the most precious things I own is a small Church of England Prayer Book that my grandmother, Anne, handed down to me. It was originally given as a gift to Anne's mother, Dorothy, from *her* mother, on the occasion of Dorothy's wedding in 1911. Mine are the fifth set of hands to hold that little heirloom. And for me, the book has become a symbol of the "big picture" worldview which stands behind the wisdom of my ancestors. I imagine my great-grandmother carrying it to church on her wedding day, and reading aloud its prayers and liturgy—her human response to the words of the Bible that she would have heard in church that day.

Ours is the first generation in the West that has not been taught the Bible. My parents, as they grew up, were handed down a thorough knowledge of the Bible. Even though they chose to reject Christianity as young adults and stopped reading the Bible, they still lived in a society which was shaped by its values. In a fascinating book called *The Book that Made Your World: How the Bible Created the Soul of Western Civilization*, Indian historian Vishal Mangalwadi traces the development of key Western values, such as the freedom and dignity of humanity, the value of science and technology, universal education, heroism, integrity, and compassion back to their origins in biblical Christianity. He demonstrates why these values arose out of a Christian worldview, and no other.

In another recent book, *The Great Bible Swindle . . . And What Can Be Done About It,* Greg Clarke argues convincingly that in the West, we need to know the Bible simply in order to understand our own language, literature, art, and culture. But he laments that ours is the first generation to be "swindled" out of such an education.

The passing on of the ancient wisdom of the Bible has all but petered out. Most of my friends seem to think that, as a society, we have outgrown Christianity. Many of them have strong beliefs about what is wrong with the Bible, Christians, and their message. But are we in danger of cutting off the branch we are sitting on? Our parents' generation at least read and studied the Bible, before many of them chose to reject it. But our generation often rejects Christianity out of hand, without ever having read the Bible for ourselves.

About four years ago, we were struggling to manage an emotional two-and-a-half year old and a newborn baby. I spent my days battling with a toddler who would not comply, and a baby who would not sleep. I remember the dread that would slowly rise in me as the sun went down. I feared that the hours of broken sleep ahead would not be enough to refuel me for another day in the ring. I was an anxious, sleep-deprived mess, desperate for guidance. But when I looked online for advice about parenting, it only confused me even more. To make matters worse, Daniel and I never seemed to agree on how to improve our situation.

It was then that I decided to reach for the ancient wisdom of my ancestors. I figured that generations of parents before me had grown up seeing the world, and their children, through the lens of Christianity. So I resolved to read through the Bible from start to finish and find out exactly what it had to say to parents like me. It took me a whole year, but I did it. And what I found was more than I had bargained for. I went looking for little pieces of grandmotherly advice, but the Bible gave me something much bigger. It gave me a grand vision—a "big picture"—which has put my life and my role as a parent into perspective. As I read, I found that the daily story of our little family began to sink into the strong embrace of a much bigger story; a story that began "in the beginning" and stretches into eternity.

Do We Really Need another Parenting Book?

My grandmother has rightly warned me that reading too many parenting books and articles will only serve to undermine my confidence. When she was raising young children, the only source of advice my Granny had were the letters her mother wrote. Her mother's parenting philosophy was simple, but brilliant: "Do your best."

So why am I now adding to the mass of information that parents probably shouldn't be reading? Because if we want to make sense of all the advice we hear, we need to have a big picture. This book will not fill your mind with hundreds of new parenting strategies that you *should* implement immediately. I trust that after reading this book, you will have the confidence to make those day-to-day parenting decisions for yourself. Rather, reading this book will help you to soar high above the "parenting wars" and controversies and to see your role from a new perspective. Once you have the big picture in mind, you can choose to home in on whatever information and advice supports your aims and values, and confidently disregard the rest.

As we explore the story of the Bible, my hope is that you will become a "big picture parent" who:

- Knows your purpose in life and parenthood
- Accepts your human limitations
- Does not parent out of guilt or fear
- Knows your family's values
- Strives to pass your values onto your children
- Strengthens your family's structure
- Sees your family as part of a wider community

My frame was not hidden from you
> when I was made in the secret place,
> when I was woven together in the depths of the earth.

Your eyes saw my unformed body;
> all the days ordained for me were written in your book
> before one of them came to be. (Psalm 139:13-16)

God knows every child, even in the womb, and has a plan for his or her life. This is what God said to one young person, the prophet Jeremiah, "Before I formed you in the womb I knew you, before you were born I set you apart; I appointed you as a prophet to the nations" (Jeremiah 1:5).

All people, including children, are made to honor God and love other people. One Bible writer spells this out in his prayer to God, saying, "From the lips of children and infants you have ordained praise" (Psalm 8:2). There are also many instances in the Bible where children are the "heroes"—the ones who demonstrate a love for God and other people—often to the shame of the adults around them. Some examples are Samuel (1 Samuel 3), Naaman's servant girl (2 Kings 5:1-15), the young David (1 Samuel 17), and King Josiah (2 Kings 22). Being young does not disqualify children from living out their big purpose in the world.

But What about Happiness?

We have seen that God did not make humans *primarily* to be happy, but rather to rule creation, to honor him, and to love others. However, God promises that living out our Big Purpose will, in turn, bring us great satisfaction.

The book of Ecclesiastes follows one man's search for meaning in life. He tries to find meaning and satisfaction in everything—study, wealth, hard work, and pleasure. But he realizes that all of those things are "meaningless" in themselves, because they do not last. Everyone—wise or foolish, rich or poor—dies in the end. He concludes:

Now all has been heard;
> here is the conclusion of the matter:

Fear God and keep his commandments,
> for this is the duty of all mankind. (Ecclesiastes 12:13)

Honoring God and keeping his commands (including his command to love others) is what gives meaning to all that we do. Elsewhere, the writer puts it like this:

> A person can do nothing better than to eat and drink and find satisfaction in their own toil. This too, I see, is from the hand of God, for without him, who can eat or find enjoyment? To the person who pleases him, God gives wisdom, knowledge and happiness, but to the sinner he gives the task of gathering and storing up wealth to hand it over to the one who pleases God. This too is meaningless, a chasing after the wind. (Ecclesiastes 2:24-26)

Without reference to God, our search for happiness will only end in frustration. But when we live our lives to his glory, we will find true meaning and satisfaction. Israel's most famous King, David, put it this way:

> Trust in the Lord and do good;
>> dwell in the land and enjoy safe pasture.
>
> Take delight in the Lord,
>> and he will give you the desires of your heart. (Psalm 37:1-4)

We live in a world which urges us to chase after the things that make us feel good. As parents, we want to protect our children from feeling unhappy. But current research confirms what the Bible has been saying all along—that happiness makes a wonderful long-term by-product, but an impossible short-term goal.

Realizing that I could not make my children happy shook the very foundations of my parenting. It forced me to step back and see the bigger picture. We and our children were made for more than happiness—we were made to be in relationship with God, his creation, and each other. Parenting is not about helping my children to *feel* good, but to *do* the good that they were created to do. And ironically, doing this—giving my children a sense of purpose and connection to God, creation, and others—is actually the best way to help them find lasting happiness.

2

The Purpose of Parenthood: Aiming for More Than Bedtime

OUR ELDEST SON STARTED school last year; and so we have been initiated into the ritual of the daily school pick-up. It is a strange sort of routine—standing around with the same group of parents each day, thinking, "Here we are again!" We have more or less the same conversation every day: "How are you? How are the kids? What did you do today?"

Sometimes I doubt whether anyone actually wants to know what I have been doing since the morning drop-off. I feel bored just talking about it. "Well, I took my younger sons to do the grocery shopping, then we went home for so-and-so's nap, then I cleaned up the breakfast things, washed some clothes, prepared lunch, hung the clothes out to dry . . . do you really want me to go on?"

Family life is very repetitive—each day seems like part of an endless cycle of keeping small people dressed, fed, cleaned, and rested, until we finally collapse into bed ourselves. And soon enough, the sun rises, and it starts all over again. And before you know it, days turn into weeks, which turn into months; and suddenly people are telling you there are only a few weeks until Christmas again.

And yet, as I stand at the school gate, I think: surely my life must add up to more than just a daily repetition of mundane tasks. I am sure I should be aiming for something more than bedtime. But what, exactly?

In the previous chapter, we saw that humans were created in God's image for a Big Purpose: to rule creation, to honor God, and to love other people. But the Bible also has a lot to say about how this plays out in the relationship between parents and their children.

Parents Provide Children with an Enduring Bond of Love

In the Bible, God does not just talk about parenthood as an abstract concept—he *models* parenthood in action. God uses the language of fatherhood (and occasionally motherhood) to describe his own relationship with the people he has made. And the foundation of this relationship is God's love and commitment to his "children."

In the book of Hosea, we read about God's fatherly love for his "child"—the group of families he rescued from slavery in Egypt (here they are called "Israel" or "Ephraim", after their ancestors):

> When Israel was a child, I loved him,
>> and out of Egypt I called my son . . .
>
> It was I who taught Ephraim to walk,
>> taking them by the arms;
>
> but they did not realize
>> it was I who healed them.
>
> I led them with cords of human kindness,
>> with ties of love.
>
> To them I was like one who lifts
>> a little child to the cheek,
>
>> and I bent down to feed them. (Hosea 11:1, 3-4)

God was reminding his spiritual children how much he loved them and how hard he had worked to raise them.

The prophet Isaiah also used the metaphor of the parent-child relationship at a time when Israel doubted God's love and commitment to her:

> Can a mother forget the baby at her breast
>> and have no compassion on the child she has borne?
>
> Though she may forget,
>> I will not forget you!
>
> See, I have engraved you on the palms of my hands;
>> your walls are ever before me. (Isaiah 49:15-16)

> Listen to me, you descendants of Jacob,
>> all the remnant of the people of Israel,

you whom I have upheld since your birth,

and have carried since you were born.

Even to your old age and grey hairs

I am he, I am he who will sustain you.

I have made you and I will carry you;

I will sustain you and I will rescue you. (Isaiah 46:3-4)

When I am at our local shopping center, I notice many people with tattoos on their body. I find it interesting to see the different designs they have chosen. One of the most common tattoos people have is of their children's names. The bond between parents and children is one of the few relationships that seems worthy of such a permanent reminder. Maybe that is the kind of sentiment God expresses when he says he has "engraved" his children on the palms of his hands. Both in the Bible and in our experience, having children implies a lifelong bond of love and commitment to them. Next, we will see that this love begins with protecting our children's lives, as far as it depends on us.

Parenthood Is about Protecting Life

Children are valued differently in different societies. While some cultures esteem and even venerate children, others permit child labor, child marriage, or even infanticide. In some cultures, the value of a child is determined by how useful (or conversely, how burdensome) they are to their parents. In some countries, such as China and India, there is a strong cultural preference for having sons. Consequently, thousands of girls suffer from selective abortion and infanticide every year.

Our modern, Western society tends to measure a child's value by his or her abilities or potential. Unborn babies who have a disability or disease are often seen as nothing more than a burden to society. Genetic testing is celebrated as a way to eradicate certain genetic abnormalities. But currently, it can only eradicate these abnormalities by "eradicating" the fetuses who are found to have them.

In other cases, the main criterion for an unborn child's value seems to be "wantedness." If an adult wants a child, they can choose to have one "created" through various means. But if an adult does not want their unborn child, they can choose to end its life.

In the next chapter, we will see that disability, disease, poverty, and suffering are part of life in this imperfect world. However, in God's eyes, even the most disabled or unwanted child is still created in God's own image, and created for a purpose. Because of this, no one has the right to take their life away. God says, "From each human being, too, I will demand an accounting for the life of another human being" (Genesis 9:5). Elsewhere, the Bible applies this principle specifically to pregnant women and their unborn babies (Exodus 21:22-25). In cases where parents are unable to care for their children, the Bible expects that other adults in the community will foster or adopt the children (James 1:27, Esther 2:7). Children born into difficult circumstances are seen as the responsibility of the whole community of God's people.

Towards the close of the Old Testament (the first part of the Bible), God's people had turned away from him and had begun to worship the gods of the nations around them. In God's eyes, the most abhorrent example of this was when some Israelites took up the practice of sacrificing their children to these false gods. Through the prophet Ezekiel, God says:

> You slaughtered my children and sacrificed them to the idols. In all your detestable practices . . . you did not remember the days of your youth, when you were naked and bare, kicking about in your blood. (Ezekiel 16:21-22)

God calls Israel's children "my children", and deeply grieves when their parents do not protect them. He rebukes parents for forgetting that they too were once helpless newborns, completely dependent on their own parents for survival.

In contrast to this negative example, many parents in the Bible chose to dedicate their children to God, acknowledging that he was their Maker. One mother, Hannah, was so grateful that God had finally enabled her to conceive a child that she devoted her son to serve in God's temple from the time he was weaned (see 1 Samuel 1).

The Bible teaches that Jesus was God—the Maker of the entire universe—in human flesh. Despite his amazing power, as a baby, he was still vulnerable and dependent on his earthly parents to keep him safe. Mary and Joseph must have felt a huge weight of responsibility. I remember very clearly the day we took our first son home from hospital. I have never seen my husband drive as slowly as he did on the way home that day! We were now carrying very precious cargo.

The Bible assumes that parents will also protect their children's lives by providing the basic necessities of food, shelter, and clothing, as far as it depends on them (this is taken for granted in Matthew 7:9-11 and 2 Corinthians 12:14). In ancient times, nuclear families were usually part of a wider community, which would help them to do this when times were tough.

The Bible argues that every child is valuable because they are made in the image of God, their Maker. Consequently, adults are responsible for protecting a child's life, as far as it depends on them.

Parenthood Is about Passing On Values

Throughout human history, it was assumed that the family (with the support of the wider community) was the place where children would naturally imbibe the worldview and values of their parents. This was true of the community of God's people described in the Bible. Notice how the prophet Moses encouraged parents to work hard to pass on key instructions to their children:

> Hear, O Israel: the Lord our God, the Lord is one. Love the Lord your God with all your heart and with all your soul and with all your strength. These commandments that I give you today are to be on your hearts. Impress them on your children. Talk about them when you sit at home and when you walk along the road, when you lie down and when you get up. (Deuteronomy 6:4-7)

In today's world, this responsibility is not always recognized. I have heard some parents say that they do not want to teach their children any kind of religious belief, so that their children can make up their own mind when they are old enough. That sounds very noble, but the reality is that children do establish their basic understanding of the world when they are young. You can see this in their constant questions about the world. It is our role to answer their questions as best we can, according to our own beliefs. Our children may go on to reject some of those beliefs as adults, but we parents are the ones who lay the foundations, and we have a responsibility to do this well.

We seem to be witnessing a gradual shift of responsibility when it comes to teaching values to our children. One day, I was shocked to read this line in our son's preschool newsletter: "It is our job as educators to teach your children about healthy eating. We would appreciate your support in this by avoiding unhealthy food in their lunches." Surely it is the preschool's job to support us, the parents—not the other way around! On another occasion, I was talking to a mother at preschool. At the beginning of the year, her son's teacher had expressed some concern that he was displaying some "antisocial" behaviors. At the end of the year, she was frustrated to hear the teacher reiterate the same concern. She asked the teacher, "So what have you been doing about it?" More and more, schools are expected to take on the responsibility for teaching values which have traditionally been taught in the home.

On a very pragmatic level, children grow up to replace their parents in the world; it is our role to show them how to be the kind of people we want them to be once we are no longer here.

Parenthood Is about Helping Children Reach Moral Maturity

The Bible considers children to be fully human—people with a Big Purpose—from the moment they are conceived. They are created to honor God and love others, just like adults. But the Bible also observes that children mature in stages, both physically and in a moral sense.

Consequently, the Bible seems to imply that very young children rely completely on their parents for moral guidance; they need our help to know how to live out their purpose. In Deuteronomy 1:39, children are called those "who do not yet know good from bad." Similarly, when Israel's famous King Solomon ascended to the throne, he prayed this prayer to God, describing himself as a little child, who needed guidance:

> Now, Lord my God, you have made your servant [that is, Solomon himself] king in place of my father David. But I am only a little child and do not know how to carry out my duties. Your servant is here among the people you have chosen, a great people, too numerous to count or number. So give your servant a discerning heart to govern your people and to distinguish between right and wrong. (1 Kings 3:7-9a)

One of the ultimate aims of our parenting is to raise children who are eventually able to make their own good moral choices. When they are very young and do not yet know how to "reject the wrong and choose the right" (Isaiah 7:15), parents act like an external conscience, guiding their behavior. As they mature, they will gradually internalize the values that we have modeled and taught.

In Jewish tradition, children reach a certain level of moral responsibility at the age of twelve (for girls) or thirteen (for boys). At this age, they become a "son/daughter of the commandment" in their own right; they are old enough to choose the good and reject the bad. As this rite of passage is celebrated, a child's father even says a prayer to thank God for releasing him from his moral responsibility for the child's actions.

Interestingly, the historian Luke records an incident which occurred when Jesus was twelve years old. After celebrating the Jewish Passover festival with his extended family, Jesus stayed behind in the temple in Jerusalem without his parents' knowledge. When Mary and Joseph eventually found him there, they had the following conversation:

> His mother said to him, "Son, why have you treated us like this? Your father and I have been anxiously searching for you."
> "Why were you searching for me?" he asked. "Didn't you know I had to be in my Father's house?" But they did not understand what he was saying to them.
> Then he went down to Nazareth with them and was obedient to them. But his mother treasured all these things in her heart. And Jesus grew in wisdom and stature, and in favor with God and man. (Luke 2:48-52)

Jesus had reached a certain level of moral independence from his parents by the age of twelve—he saw God as his true Father and began to focus on this relationship in a new way. But it is interesting that even as he matured towards adulthood, Jesus continued to honor and obey his earthly parents.

As we guide our children towards moral maturity, we ought to understand our children's capabilities at each stage so that we can know when to start letting them take responsibility for their own decisions. I sometimes imagine that there is an invisible leash between me and my sons. The older they get, the longer the leash I let them have. Right now, our youngest is going through the most frightening stage—he has learnt to walk, run, and climb, but is not yet old enough to keep himself safe. When we are out, I have to keep no more than a couple of steps away, so that I can stop him from falling down stairs, knocking over a cup of hot tea, or stepping onto a road. But as he gets older, I will be able to give him a little more "leash." I think it is similar in the moral realm—as our children grow older and wiser, we gradually give them more "leash" to make their own decisions.

The key concept here is that children are people on the path towards adulthood. They will always sit somewhere on the scale from the complete dependence of a newborn to the complete independence of an adult. Parents are responsible for helping them move towards maturity in every area, including the development of a healthy morality.

Parenthood Is about Helping Children Reach Physical Maturity

While the Bible is clear about the role of parents in their children's moral development, it leaves a lot of room for movement when it comes to their physical development. What we expect from our children in terms of when they will reach a physical milestone, and how much *we* are responsible to get them there, is largely a product of our culture.

Earlier, we saw that our children are gradually moving from dependence to independence in different aspects of their lives. And when you look at some of the most hotly-debated parenting issues, the different "camps" simply locate children further up or down the scale of dependence on that particular issue. They also disagree on the extent to which parents are responsible for moving their children along. For example, some people think that babies are naturally dependent on their parents to get to sleep until they are six months or older. A corresponding belief is that parents do not need to do anything to help their children become independent sleepers. At the other end of the spectrum are those who believe that even newborns can learn the skill of self-settling, and therefore that it is their parents' job to teach them. However, by the age of five, almost all parents (in my culture) aim to have children who go to sleep in their own beds. They simply differ on when exactly they expect this to happen, and how much parents are responsible to make it happen.

You can take the same approach to almost any other parenting issue, such as eating family foods, toilet training, childcare, or household chores. When it comes to the skills of adulthood, we are all aiming for much the same thing. We just differ in our timeframe and in the extent of the responsibility we take for it. When I realized this, it took the heat out of many of the issues that can cause friction between parents. Now, when an issue comes up in our family, we simply ask ourselves: What will we expect of our children in this area by the time they are adults? At what age do we expect they will attain this skill? Are we responsible to teach it to them? If so, how can we gradually train them towards independence?

Summary of Part 1

The Bible puts the mundane story of our daily lives into a much bigger picture. We are made for more than momentary happiness. Parents and their children were made in the image of God for a Big Purpose—to rule creation, to honor our Maker, and to love other people. Children share this purpose, even from the womb. The purpose of parenthood is not only to conceive and give birth to children, but to protect their life, pass on our values, and guide them towards moral and physical maturity. In this way, we help our children to live out their God-given purpose on earth.

The story of how God created humanity for a Big Purpose sounds simple enough. God made Adam and Eve to live in a beautiful world; they got married, had two kids, and lived happily ever after . . . right? Sadly, that is not how the story went for them; and that is not how the story goes for us, either. To truly understand the world we and our children live in, and how this world shapes our understanding of parenthood, we need to keep reading.

Enter "Sin"

Genesis 1–2 painted an idyllic picture: Adam and Eve were living out God's Big Purpose for them in the Garden of Eden—honoring God, caring for his creation and sharing a loving relationship with each other. God, like a good Father, provided everything that they needed. But for their good, God gave them one restriction—they were not to eat fruit from the "tree of the knowledge of good and evil."

Why didn't God want Adam and Eve to eat from this tree? The Bible certainly sees wisdom—knowing good from evil, and choosing the good—as a positive thing. However, this wisdom is only considered good on one condition: if it comes from God. In the words of the wise King Solomon, "The fear of the Lord is the beginning of wisdom" (Proverbs 9:10). That means that true wisdom starts with giving God the honor (sometimes called "fear" in Bible times) that he deserves as our Maker. The opposite of this is to be "wise in your own eyes" (Proverbs 3:7). God wanted Adam and Eve to look to him alone for moral guidance.

At this point in the narrative, we meet the serpent, or Satan, who embodies all that stands opposed to God. Satan is called the "father of lies" (John 8:44), because he seeks to deceive people into seeking happiness apart from God's purposes for them. As the story unfolds, the serpent seeks to undermine Adam and Eve's trust in God's good reason for giving them that one prohibition. Adam and Eve choose to trust the serpent's lies rather than their Creator's word—they eat the fruit of the forbidden tree. The Bible then describes the consequences of their sin—their act of rebellion against God's loving authority:

> So the Lord God said to the serpent, "Because you have done this,
> "Cursed are you above all livestock
>   and all wild animals!
> You will crawl on your belly
>   and you will eat dust
>   all the days of your life.
> And I will put enmity
>   between you and the woman,
>   and between your offspring and hers;
> he will crush your head,
>   and you will strike his heel."

To the woman he said,

"I will make your pains in childbearing very severe;

> with painful labor you will give birth to children.

Your desire will be for your husband,

> and he will rule over you."

To Adam he said, "Because you listened to your wife and ate fruit from the tree about which I commanded you, 'You must not eat from it,'

"Cursed is the ground because of you;

> through painful toil you will eat food from it

> all the days of your life.

It will produce thorns and thistles for you,

> and you will eat the plants of the field.

By the sweat of your brow

> you will eat your food

until you return to the ground,

> since from it you were taken;

for dust you are

> and to dust you will return." (Genesis 3:14-19)

Adam and Eve's act of sin (sometimes called the "fall of humanity") had consequences for all of humanity's key relationships—our relationships with God, creation, and each other. Adam and Eve still had a mandate to fill the earth and rule over it, but carrying this out would become difficult. Bearing children would now be painful, harvesting food from the earth would now be frustrating, and marriage would now be characterized by envy and domination. Humanity would also face an ongoing struggle with the serpent's lies. The final consequence of sin was that God banished Adam and Eve from the Garden of Eden, cutting off their access to the "tree of life": life outside the Garden of Eden would be marred by sickness, ageing, and death.

It is into this "fallen" world that the first children were born. Eve went on to give birth to two sons, Cain and Abel. Adam and Eve probably had high hopes for their sons—maybe they would overcome the serpent's lies and stay true to their Big Purpose on earth. Abel did honor God, which he expressed by his heartfelt worship. However, this only provoked Cain to envy:

THE LIMITS OF BEING HUMAN: OUR GUILT AND FEAR

> Then the Lord said to Cain, "Why are you angry? Why is your face downcast? If you do what is right, will you not be accepted? But if you do not do what is right, sin is crouching at your door; it desires to have you, but you must rule over it."
>
> Now Cain said to his brother Abel, "Let's go out to the field." While they were in the field, Cain attacked his brother Abel and killed him. (Genesis 4:6-8)

God made people for relationship, but he gave us the freedom to conduct these relationships however we choose. God does not force us to honor him or to love others—he wants us to do those things of our own free will. By eating the forbidden fruit, Adam and Eve chose to assert their independence from God and his moral standards. But they went on to experience the dark side of this freedom—they saw their own son choose envy, anger, and violence. The Bible teaches that ever since then, sin "crouches at the door" of every generation and, without fail, each generation chooses it. Each of us has inherited the sinful tendencies of our first parents.

Many people find the Bible's teaching about human sinfulness—that every single one of us inherits our first parents' "sin gene"—very confronting. However, it is not only Christians who find that this teaching rings true. Atheist philosopher Alain de Boton writes:

> Enlightenment thinkers believed that they were doing us a favour by declaring man to be originally and naturally good. However, being repeatedly informed of our native decency can cause us to become paralysed with remorse over our failure to measure up to impossible standards of integrity. Confessions of universal sinfulness turn out to be a better starting point from which to take our first modest steps towards virtue.[1]

If all of us are inherently sinful, this has significant implications for our understanding of our role as parents. Let's look at them now.

I Am Not Perfect: Accepting My Mixed Impact

The first implication of the fall of humanity is that I cannot expect perfection from myself.

Last year, we went to my father-in-law's sixtieth birthday party in the town where my husband grew up. And there was a very special moment when one of Daniel's primary school teachers saw him for the first time in

1. De Boton, *Religion for Atheists*, chapter 3, part 7, para. 4.

decades. She was talking to Daniel, but she kept looking down at our eldest son in amazement. She said it was like looking back in time and seeing Daniel, as she remembered him. If she had spent more time with us, she probably would have noticed some similarities in their personalities and interests too.

The Bible describes the birth of Adam and Eve's third child like this:

> When God created mankind, he made them in the likeness of God. He created them male and female and blessed them. And he named them "Mankind" when they were created.
>
> When Adam had lived 130 years, he had a son in his own likeness, in his own image; and he named him Seth. (Genesis 5:1-3)

For better or worse, our children are stamped with our "image." Who we are and what we do will inevitably affect them. Just as our children might inherit our big nose or curly hair, they also inherit (by "nature" and "nurture") our character traits—both the virtues and the vices.

When we come to terms with the fact that, as human parents, we cannot avoid having both a positive and a negative impact on our children, it can free us from much of the guilt which we experience about our parenting. Psychologist, Judith Locke, observes:

> Guilty feelings are often backed up by two faulty beliefs that are becoming ingrained in our society. The first is that perfect parenting is possible and desirable; the other is that children will not recover from difficult events or tricky situations . . . Unfortunately, it is the parent's long, guilty memory of their past minor or unavoidable "mistakes" that produces parental worry and distress. It can sometimes encourage an indulgent type of parenting that . . . is not in the best interests of the child.[2]

A revolutionary concept we need to embrace is that of the "good enough parent."[3] Our imperfections are not just a liability—they are also an excellent opportunity to show our children how to navigate real life in this fallen world. (The Bible also offers us a way to be fully released from all of our guilt—that will be the topic of the next chapter.)

Even though children are naturally impacted by their parent's imperfections, the Bible does not portray humans as trapped by their upbringing—we are not victims of our parents' mistakes. Part of the task

---

2. Locke, *Bonsai Child*, chapter 2, section 6, para. 5, 7.

3. Oates outlines the history of this phrase in Oates, 20 *Tips*, Introduction, para 5.

of maturing as a person is to evaluate which of our parents' beliefs and behaviors we want to bring with us into adulthood. The same will be true for the next generation. The Bible encourages children to honor and obey their parents, as a general rule (Exodus 20:12). Yet sometimes, God also says, "Do not be like your parents" (2 Chronicles 30:7). All of us were raised by imperfect parents, and all of us, as adults, have to take responsibility for how we move forward from that. In the next chapter, we will see that God invites all people to become his spiritual children. As we experience his *perfect* fatherhood—his love, guidance, and empowerment—we can gradually find healing for the wounds caused by our own parents' imperfections.

The prophet Ezekiel taught about God's view of personal responsibility. At that time, people had begun to think that children paid for their parents' sin. Ezekiel used the hypothetical example of a family where a "righteous man, who does what is just and right" has a "violent son, who sheds blood", who, in turn, has a son "who sees all the sins his father commits, and though he sees them, he does not do such things" (Ezekiel 18:5-18). Ezekiel concludes: "The child will not share the guilt of the parent, nor will the parent share the guilt of the child. The righteousness of the righteous will be credited to them, and the wickedness of the wicked will be charged against them" (Ezekiel 18:20).

God holds each person accountable for their own actions. Neither parents nor children are held accountable for the actions of the other. As parents, we are held accountable to God for how *we* act as a parent, but we are not held responsible for the actions of our children—neither the good nor the bad. We do have a significant impact on our children; in fact, most of this book is about how to have a positive impact on them. However, a time will come when it is up to them to choose their path, and God will hold them alone responsible for what they choose.

There is freedom for those who embrace the biblical teaching that as parents, we can never attain perfection. Our sin and imperfections will impact our children, but they will not determine their future. What a relief!

My Children Are Not Perfect: Accepting Their Mixed Response

The second implication of raising children in a fallen world is that, like us, our children are not perfect. This can be particularly hard for modern parents to admit.

My mother-in-law has been a teacher for almost thirty years. She and her colleagues have noticed a significant change in the attitudes of parents in recent years. In the past, when a child misbehaved, parents would generally feel ashamed of what happened, apologize to the teacher, and follow up with some kind of consequence for their child at home. But many of today's parents simply cannot admit that their child has done the wrong thing. They try to excuse the child's behavior, defend them, or even blame the teacher. As modern parents, we can find it hard to accept that our children make mistakes.

But really, our children's imperfections should not come as a surprise. Children are just like adults, in that they have inherited Adam and Eve's tendency to claim autonomy from God and his moral standards. King David confessed, "Surely I was sinful at birth, sinful from the time my mother conceived me" (Psalm 51:5). No one has to teach a child to disobey us with a "no!" or "mine"! Children are not born morally neutral, but with the inclination to focus on their needs and desires at the expense of others'.

Adam and Eve were free to choose whether they would honor God and love other people, and so were their children. Experts like to claim that "if you do X, your children will do Y," but there are no guarantees. In a similar way, many Christians quote the biblical proverb, "Train a child in the way he should go, and when he is old he will not turn from it" (Proverbs 22:6). But the Book of Proverbs is not a book of rigid formulas for life. Rather, it is a treasury of observations about how life *usually* works, based on common human experiences. Wise parents do diligently "train" their children, but the other parts of the Bible point to the reality that no one can guarantee how the child will respond. We can faithfully do our part (with plenty of mistakes along the way), but the rest is out of our hands.

I have often asked my grandmothers about how they raised my parents and their siblings, hoping to work out the perfect formula. But they usually respond rather frustratingly with something like, "Actually, I can't really remember. I just did what I thought was right at the time and hoped for the best." No one can ever guarantee the result of their parenting "experiment."

The Bible gives examples of all kinds of families. Some children grow up to reflect their parents' character and values—they "turn out right"—but some children don't. In the Old Testament, we have the example of Daniel and his three friends, who were taken captive as young men and trained to serve the King of Babylon. These young men faithfully lived out the values they had learned at home, even when it brought them into conflict with the laws of the foreign country where they served. On several occasions, they risked their lives to stand firm in the faith they had inherited.

By contrast, Jesus told the famous parable of the Prodigal Son:

> Jesus continued: "There was a man who had two sons. The younger one said to his father, 'Father, give me my share of the estate.' So he divided his property between them.
>
> "Not long after that, the younger son got together all he had, set off for a distant country and there squandered his wealth in wild living. After he had spent everything, there was a severe famine in that whole country, and he began to be in need. So he went and hired himself out to a citizen of that country, who sent him to his fields to feed pigs. He longed to fill his stomach with the pods that the pigs were eating, but no one gave him anything." (Luke 15:11-16)

It is interesting that the Father in this story (who represents God) did not stop his son from leaving. The Father let his son make his own moral decisions, even though he knew they would lead him into trouble. In the same way, there will come an age where our children are responsible for their own decisions and actions. At that point, we will have to trust that we have done our best, and let them go.

My Children's World Is Not Perfect: Accepting a Mixed Environment

The third implication of living in a fallen world is that I am not in control over my children's lives—I cannot stop bad things from happening. Despite all the advances in science and technology, so much about the process of having children is still out of our hands. For starters, we cannot control how long it takes to conceive, whether it is a boy or a girl, when the baby will arrive, or whether he or she will be healthy. In the Bible, one desperate woman, Rachel, says to her husband, "Give me children, or I'll die!" But her husband is aware of his human limitations and simply responds with, "Am I in the place of God, who has kept you from having children?" (Genesis 30:1-2).

The natural processes of conception and childbirth have also been marred by the fall of humanity, as we saw earlier in Genesis 3:16. Ever since then, having children has been difficult, painful, and dangerous. The Bible candidly includes stories of women who struggled with infertility, had miscarriages, or even died in childbirth. Infertile Rachel actually did go on to have children; but tragically, this is how her story ended:

> While they were still some distance from Ephrath, Rachel began to give birth and had great difficulty. And as she was having great difficulty in childbirth, the midwife said to her, "Don't despair, for you have another son." As she breathed her last—for she was dying—she named her son Ben-Oni. But his father named him Benjamin. (Genesis 35:16-18)

Trusting in the natural processes that God has designed is a good starting point when it comes to giving birth to children. More and more, science is uncovering just how intricately the processes of conception, birth and breastfeeding are designed; human intervention certainly carries significant risks. But in this imperfect world, even natural conception, birth and breastfeeding can go wrong. Because of these dangers and difficulties, the Bible considers "pregnant women and nursing mothers" to be among the most vulnerable people in times of trouble (see Matthew 24:19).

Of course, we do our very best to keep ourselves and our children safe as they come into the world. In the West, we are thankfully supported in this by advanced modern medicine. But ever since the fall of humanity, childbirth has been a risky process. This fact became tragically real in our family five years ago. Daniel's youngest sister had gone into labor with her first child and we were waiting excitedly for news. But late that night, the phone rang and the news was not good. My sister-in-law had given birth to a healthy baby boy. But following the birth, she had had some rare, but serious complications—Jacque died just hours after becoming a mother. Sometimes we still can't believe that it really happened—she was in a state-of-the-art hospital right here in Australia.

For us in the modern West, it is a shock to realize that we are not in control of the process of having children. And then, after our children have safely arrived into the world, we are faced with another difficult truth: we cannot prevent bad things from happening to them.

Lenore Skenazy famously became "America's Worst Mom" when she allowed her nine-year-old son to ride the New York subway home on his own (at his request). She had to publicly defend her decision in the face of what she calls "the impossible obsession of our era: total safety for our children every second of every day."[4] It is a good thing that the world has become a safer place for children. But all the emphasis on safety deceives

---

4. Skenazy, *Free Range Kids*, Introduction, section 5, para. 1.

us into thinking that we can always stop our children from getting hurt or sick; that we can prevent anything bad from ever happening to them. When we do have to let our children go where we cannot protect them, we can feel afraid because we are not in control any more. It is this fear that turns some of us into "helicopter parents."

Last year, there was an outbreak of whooping cough at our son's school. Every day, we were notified of a new reported case. And it was hard to keep sending our little boy along without worrying, especially since we had a new baby at home. (We had all been immunized against whooping cough, but that seemed to be no guarantee.) I found myself fastidiously washing our son's hands when he came home from school each day and quizzing him about whether his classmates had been coughing. Sending a child into a school full of whooping cough germs is a good illustration for what it feels like to bring children into this imperfect world—we are helplessly out of control.

The Bible is honest about the fact that in this world, parents cannot always keep their children safe and well. Some children are born with disabilities, some get sick, and some even die before their parents, like the children of King David (2 Samuel 12:16-23) and Job (Job 1:18-22). In this imperfect world, children can lose their parents too. The book of Esther tells the story of a young girl who lost both parents and was brought up by a cousin.

Jesus recognized the pain that parents feel when they cannot provide a safe environment for their children. When he predicted that Jerusalem was about to be crushed by Roman forces, Jesus said, "Daughters of Jerusalem, do not weep for me; weep for yourselves and for your children. For the time will come when you will say, 'Blessed are the childless women, the wombs that never bore and the breasts that never nursed!'" (Luke 23:28-29). Sometimes the pain of seeing our children experience the hard things in this life is almost too much to bear—so much so, that it could even be considered better not to have children in the first place.

The End of Imperfection

The Bible's story is not just about the present, but the future. It promises that a day will come when God will reverse the effects of the fall of humanity—there will be no more guilt, fear, pain, death, or sadness for those who belong to God. The Bible foresees a time when people will be able

45

to live with God once again—just like Adam and Eve did in the Garden of Eden—because he has washed away all of their sin and imperfection. The Bible calls this future "the new heavens and the new earth" or heaven. God's people will get to experience this new reality when Jesus comes back to earth as King (or after we die, if that happens first). Importantly, heaven will be a place where we will no longer have to fear for our children's safety. It is a place where:

> The wolf will live with the lamb,
>> the leopard will lie down with the goat,
> the calf and the lion and the yearling together;
>> and a little child will lead them.
> The cow will feed with the bear,
>> their young will lie down together,
>> and the lion will eat straw like the ox.
> The infant will play near the cobra's den,
>> and the young child will put its hand into the viper's nest.
> They will neither harm nor destroy
>> on all my holy mountain,
> for the earth will be filled with the knowledge of the Lord
>> as the waters cover the sea. (Isaiah 11:6-9)

The reality of life in this fallen world makes being a parent very difficult—we are constantly confronted with the Big Problem of our human limitations. Our own mistakes and shortcomings can make us feel incredibly guilty and afraid of damaging our children. At other times, we watch on as our imperfect children make foolish choices and reap the consequences. We can become afraid of all the potential risks to our children in this world of sin and death. But if we are to be the parents we were created to be, we need to find a way of moving beyond our feelings of guilt and fear. How we can do that is the subject of the next chapter.

4

Parents in Need of a Parent: Finding Forgiveness and Comfort

FOR MY HUSBAND AND me, the weeks following the birth of our first child were tough. We were in a haze of exhaustion—stumbling around the house, never managing to get out, and fumbling our way through our new responsibilities. In my case, nursing was extremely painful and I dreaded every feed. I remember how proud I felt when I made it through my first whole day without crying.

All I wanted in those first weeks was someone to look after *me* and show me what to do. Faced with my overwhelming new role as a mother, I felt like a child who needed my own mum and dad. Thankfully, my parents did come around for a while—they cooked us hearty meals, helped us get out of the house, and reassured us that things would get better (which they did). But many other times since then, the challenges of being a parent have left me feeling completely lost and helpless.

As I read through the Bible, I was relieved to discover that actually, God doesn't expect us to "have it all together", even as parents. In fact, the Bible says that if we want to come to God, we have to stop being "grown-ups" and become like little children—children of God.

Parenthood makes us extremely aware of our human limitations—our Big Problem. Being imperfect parents to imperfect children in an imperfect world can leave us feeling guilty and afraid. On top of that, we often feel confused by the sea of information and advice that swirls around us. But the Bible says that when we reach the limits of our human capabilities—when we are too frail and small to be the parents we want to be—we can look up towards *our* Father in heaven and rest in his endless compassion

47

and strength. And strangely, being children of God enables us to become better parents too.

Becoming Children of God

At the time of Jesus, many people believed that to get close to God, you had to work your way up the spiritual hierarchy by keeping a set of religious rules. On one occasion, Jesus' disciples asked him who was at the top of that hierarchy. Matthew recounts Jesus' response:

> He called a little child to him, and placed the child among them. And he said: "Truly I tell you, unless you change and become like little children, you will never enter the kingdom of heaven. Therefore, whoever takes the lowly position of this child is the greatest in the kingdom of heaven." (Matthew 18:2-4)

The disciples thought that children were at the bottom of the spiritual hierarchy; after all, they have not had much time to earn their way to God. But that is just the point that Jesus was making—children show us what it is like to be needy. We can learn from them how to humble ourselves before God and depend on him. Often, we approach God with our hands full—we want to show him how hard we have tried and how good we have been. But Jesus says that we can only approach God with empty hands, like a child waiting for a gift.

In order to come to God, we have to acknowledge our Big Problem: that we have not lived up to God's purposes for us. According to the Bible, our sin—our failure to honor our Creator and love others—is serious. When Adam and Eve sinned, God banished them from the Garden of Eden and cut off their access to the tree of life. In a similar way, our sin separates us from God and the life he gives. The result of this is spiritual death. Our guilt is not just an uncomfortable feeling, but a symptom of a terminal illness.

So how can we get rid of the sin that stands between us and God? How can we be cured of our deadly disease? My natural response to my mistakes is to try harder; but the Bible says that no amount of trying can get rid of our sin. Our spiritual problem is so big that only God can fix it.

God's solution to the problem of sin came in the form of a person—Jesus. He was one of Adam and Eve's many descendants, but he was also God's beloved Son. God sent Jesus into the world as a perfect example of how to honor him and love others. The Bible describes Jesus as a "new

Adam"—one who never disobeyed God (Romans 5:12-21, 1 Corinthians 15:45-49). Jesus was the only human who had no sin to separate him from God.

And yet, Jesus was accused of blasphemy (for claiming to be God's Son) and handed over to the Romans to be executed. Jesus was crucified as a criminal, even though he had done nothing wrong. But Jesus went willingly to the cross, knowing that it was part of God's plan to save sinners. Jesus chose to take upon himself all of *our* sin and bear the consequences— death and separation from God—*for us*. Three days later, Jesus rose from the dead, proving that he had destroyed the power of sin and death forever.

Peter, an early church leader, wrote, "'He himself bore our sins' in his body on the cross, so that we might die to sins and live for righteousness; 'by his wounds you have been healed'" (1 Peter 2:24). At the cross, Jesus exchanged his sinless life for our sinful one. If we give our lives over to him, his death will count for us and we can start again with a clean bill of spiritual health. Then we will experience a spiritual "resurrection" to eternal life, just like he did.

The Bible describes this process as being "born again" or "adopted" into God's family (see John 3:3-8 and Ephesians 1:5). The apostle John wrote this about how different people responded to Jesus:

> Yet to all who did receive him, to those who believed in his name, he gave the right to become children of God—children born not of natural descent, nor of human decision or a husband's will, but born of God. (John 1:12-13)

If we humble ourselves like little children, we can become children of God, the only perfect parent. The Bible describes God as the epitome of fatherhood; he is the one "from whom all fatherhood in heaven and on earth derives its name" (Ephesians 3:15). In the Bible, God is occasionally described in motherly terms too (for example, Job 38:28-29 and Matthew 23:37). In a sense, God incorporates both parental roles, even though the Bible usually describes him in masculine terms.

There are many different kinds of fathers, so this begs the question— what kind of father is God?

In recent years, I have read quite a few parenting books written by psychologists, doctors, and teachers. Surprisingly, they all have the same basic message: the most effective parents are those who are both warm *and* firm towards their children; they avoid the extremes of being permissive (all warmth) or authoritarian (all firmness).[1] These parents have a strong relationship with their children—they know them and love them unconditionally. However, they also set strong boundaries around their children's behavior. These parents take responsibility for helping their children to reach physical and moral maturity. It is no surprise to find that this is exactly how the Bible describes God, the perfect parent—as a model of unconditional love and clear expectations.

Surely the best way to become a better parent is to experience the perfect parenting of God!

God's Perfect Fatherhood: Unconditional Love

We can see evidence of God's unconditional love in three areas: his acceptance of us, no matter what; his provision for us; and his attention to us.

God Accepts Me as I Am

These days, there is a lot of talk about self-esteem—our society tries to make us feel good about ourselves all the time. But the Bible's honest assessment of me provides a much stronger foundation for my self-worth than simply telling myself that I am OK. The Bible tells me that I am not at all OK—I have sinned against my Maker and there is nothing I can do to make it right again. However, at the same time, right now, just as I am, I am deeply loved by God; he has made a way to forgive me through Jesus and change me for the better.

As parents, this more complex view of ourselves—sinful, but always loved by God—frees us to be honest about our failings and our need for grace, rather than trying to maintain a facade of perfection—both in front of God and in front of our children. We can also help our children to acknowledge that they make bad choices sometimes too. And just like God, we can reassure our children that they are forgiven and loved, by us and by God, no matter what.

Psychologists believe that many modern parents have misunderstood the concept of self-esteem—they think it's about making their children feel good all the time by lowering their expectations to make sure that their

---

1 Locke, *Bonsai Child*, chapter 2, section 1, part 3, para. 5; Oates, 20 *Tips*, chapter 5, section 7, para. 1-2; Palmer, *Toxic Childhood*, chapter 10, section 1, para. 2-3.

children never fail, while simultaneously praising them for being awesome, amazing, talented, and clever.[2] But ironically, this eventually leads to poor self-confidence when children realize that their successes were "staged" by well-meaning adults, rather than the result of their own abilities and efforts. Psychologists are urging parents to remember that true self-esteem comes from children learning how to persevere, in spite of their failures and disappointments.[3]

This fits in well with the Bible's assessment of our human nature: we are flawed and make mistakes—sometimes very serious ones—but as God's dearly loved children, we can be forgiven and redeemed to live out our Big Purpose.

The Bible rings with the truth that God loves his children, no matter what. Paul writes, "God demonstrates his own love for us in this: While we were still sinners, Christ died for us" (Romans 5:8). Jesus illustrated this in his parable of the Prodigal Son, which we began to read in chapter 3. In this story, a father's youngest son asks for his inheritance money, then moves to a foreign country where he spends it all on momentary pleasures. Having hit rock bottom, he finally decides to return home to his father.

My husband and I met a real life "prodigal" a few years ago, when we were driving home after an evening out. As we turned into our street, our headlights caught the reflection of a large shiny suitcase. We could just make out the shape of a girl sitting beside it; she was crying. We parked the car and went over. The girl said her name was Rochelle and she was looking for her dad's house; in the dark, she had lost her way. She said she had just broken up with her long-term boyfriend and had nowhere else to go. Rochelle's dad had not approved of their relationship, so she hadn't spoken to him in years.

We managed to call Rochelle's dad and organized to meet him at a car park (parking lot) a few blocks away. On the way, Rochelle kept repeating that her father was going to be extremely angry with her—she had been stubborn, disrespectful, and rebellious. In the end, he had been right about the boyfriend. When we got to the car park, we got out and waited anxiously for a few minutes. Suddenly, out of the darkness, a white van screeched around the corner and pulled in sharply beside us. The door opened and a man came out, running towards us. We did not know what would happen next.

---

2. Locke, *Bonsai Child*, chapter 2, section 1, part 2, para. 2-5, Sax, *Collapse of Parenting*, chapter 8, para. 6-8.

3. Locke, *Bonsai Child*, chapter 2, section 1, part 2, para. 5.

Rochelle's father ran to his daughter and took her in his arms; both of them were crying. It was not the angry reunion Rochelle had feared, but one of the most tender moments I have ever witnessed. Her father was just so relieved to have his daughter back after all those years.

That is what happened at the end of Jesus' parable too. The Father, who represents God, ran to his remorseful son, who represents all human sinners, and embraced him, saying, "Let's have a feast and celebrate. For this son of mine was dead and is alive again; he was lost and is found" (Luke 15:23-24).

Unconditional love, expressed in forgiveness, lies at the heart of our relationship with God and our role as parents. Almost one thousand years before Jesus, King David described God like this:

> The Lord is compassionate and gracious,
>
> > slow to anger, abounding in love.
>
> He will not always accuse,
>
> > nor will he harbor his anger for ever;
>
> he does not treat us as our sins deserve
>
> > or repay us according to our iniquities.
>
> For as high as the heavens are above the earth,
>
> > so great is his love for those who fear him;
>
> as far as the east is from the west,
>
> > so far has he removed our transgressions from us.
>
> As a father has compassion on his children,
>
> > so the Lord has compassion on those who fear him;
>
> for he knows how we are formed,
>
> > he remembers that we are dust. (Psalm 103:8-14)

Children of God experience his unconditional fatherly love—God accepts us, no matter what, because Jesus has paid the price of our sin.

God Provides for Me

God's love for his children also involves providing for them. Jesus spoke about this in his famous Sermon on the Mount:

> So do not worry, saying, "What shall we eat?" or "What shall we drink?" or "What shall we wear?" For the pagans run after all these

> things, and your heavenly Father knows that you need them. But
> seek first his kingdom and his righteousness, and all these things
> will be given to you as well. (Matthew 6:31-33)

Children of God do not need to worry about tomorrow, because God knows their needs and can provide for them. For human parents, too, having children implies a commitment to providing them with the basic necessities of life, as far as it depends on us. I cannot even begin to imagine the heartache of parents in places where conflict or poverty make it difficult to provide food, clean water, and shelter for their children. Although human parents may at times be unable to provide for our children's needs, God is never unable, or unwilling. This is one way he demonstrates his fatherly love for us.

Interestingly, God often provides for those who are in need *through* his other children. In the Bible, God repeatedly commands his people to be generous towards the poor living among them (Leviticus 25:35, Romans 12:13, Galatians 2:10). The book of Ruth tells the moving story of how God provided for two poor widows through a generous relative.

God Listens to Me

Another expression of God's love for his children is that he listens to them when they speak and ask him for things. Jesus reminded his disciples that prayer is not primarily a religious activity, but a relational one, like a child talking to his or her parent:

> But when you pray, go into your room, close the door and pray to
> your Father, who is unseen. Then your Father, who sees what is
> done in secret, will reward you. And when you pray, do not keep
> on babbling like pagans, for they think they will be heard because
> of their many words. Do not be like them, for your Father knows
> what you need before you ask him.

> This, then, is how you should pray:
> "Our Father in heaven,
> hallowed be your name,
> your kingdom come,
> your will be done,
>> on earth as it is in heaven.
> Give us today our daily bread.

And forgive us our debts,

    as we also have forgiven our debtors.

And lead us not into temptation,

    but deliver us from the evil one." (Matthew 6:5-13)

God knows the things we need; but he wants us to ask him for them in prayer. This well-known prayer highlights some key aspects of what it means to be children of God: we honor our Father and trust in him to provide for us, forgive us, and guide us.

As human parents, we can also express our love for our children by listening to them and responding wisely to their requests. In this busy and noisy world, we need to make time for real conversations with our children to find out what is going on in their lives. We can follow God's model of being willing and available to hear about and consider their needs.

God's Perfect Fatherhood: Clear Expectations

Healthy relationships between parents and children begin with unconditional love. When we forgive our children, provide for them, and take time to listen to them, it shows that we have their best interests at heart. This warmth provides the foundation for the other side of good parenting—the firmness.

God Expects Me to Grow in Love

God wants his children to grow and mature into spiritual adulthood. The writer of Hebrews contrasts this maturity with spiritual "infancy":

> In fact, though by this time you ought to be teachers, you need someone to teach you the elementary truths of God's word all over again. You need milk, not solid food! Anyone who lives on milk, being still an infant, is not acquainted with the teaching about righteousness. But solid food is for the mature, who by constant use have trained themselves to distinguish good from evil. (Hebrews 5:12-14)

Maturity for us (and for our children) means choosing to live out our Big Purpose—honoring God and loving others.

Both God the Father and Jesus, his Son, show us how to love—how to give of ourselves for the good of others. Paul explained this in his letter to the Ephesians: "Follow God's example, therefore, as dearly loved children and live a life of love, just as Christ loved us and gave himself up for us as a fragrant offering and sacrifice to God" (Ephesians 5:1-2).

Just as we seek to reflect the values of our heavenly Father, our children will naturally imitate the values they see in us. As parents, our aim is to say along with Paul, "Follow my example, as I follow the example of Christ" (1 Corinthians 11:1). In the next chapter we will look in more detail at the kind of love which characterizes the family of God and, ideally, our own family.

God kindly makes his expectations of us very clear in the Bible. It is also important for us as human parents to make sure our children know exactly what we expect of them ahead of time, rather than waiting to correct them when they get it wrong.

God Enables Me to Love as He Does, by His Spirit

Ever since sin entered the world, parents and their children have regularly fallen short of their Big Purpose. But when any of us confess our failings and trust in Jesus, we become children of God. God deals with our Big Problem. Now we have two reasons to try all over again to honor God and love others—first, because that is what we were originally created to do, and second, because that is what we have been "born again" to do. But even if we really want to, how can we possibly live up to God's expectations, when we share the sinful nature of our first parents, Adam and Eve?

Once again, God himself has provided the solution. Hundreds of years before the birth of Jesus, God made this promise through the prophet Ezekiel:

> I will sprinkle clean water on you, and you will be clean; I will cleanse you from all your impurities and from all your idols. I will give you a new heart and put a new spirit in you; I will remove from you your heart of stone and give you a heart of flesh. And I will put my Spirit in you and move you to follow my decrees and be careful to keep my laws. (Ezekiel 36:25-27)

Rules and expectations alone cannot make people moral. Knowing this, God promised to send his own Spirit, who would motivate and empower his people from within.

When the time came for Jesus to return to God after his resurrection from the dead, Jesus told his disciples to wait in Jerusalem for this "power" that God had promised (Luke 24:45-49). Not long after this, the disciples had gathered for the Jewish festival of Pentecost. During their meeting, they experienced the powerful arrival of the Holy Spirit, who enabled them to praise God in foreign languages (see Acts 2:1-13). A crowd of onlookers gathered, wondering if the disciples were actually drunk! Peter responded:

> No, this is what was spoken by the prophet Joel:
>
> "In the last days, God says,
>> I will pour out my Spirit on all people.
>
> Your sons and daughters will prophesy,
>> your young men will see visions,
>>
>> your old men will dream dreams.
>
> Even on my servants, both men and women,
>> I will pour out my Spirit in those days,
>>
>> and they will prophesy." (Acts 2:16-18)

Peter went on to tell the crowd all about how Jesus died and rose again, showing himself to be God's Son. Peter finished by saying,

> Repent and be baptized, every one of you, in the name of Jesus Christ for the forgiveness of your sins. And you will receive the gift of the Holy Spirit. The promise is for you and your children and for all who are far off—for all whom the Lord our God will call. (Acts 2:38-39)

The New Testament promises that those who trust in Jesus will be filled with God's Spirit, enabling us to love God and other people, in spite of our sinful tendencies. In this speech, Peter specifically said that this promise is not just for us, but for our children too. As parents, then, we should not just make "rules" and expect that our children will always be able to keep them. We need to help our children to connect with the Spirit of God, who gives us an inner, spiritual motivation for loving others. We and our children can ask God to help us do the right thing, by the power of his Spirit. I, for one, have to do this a lot!

Doing good by the power of the Spirit, not by our human effort alone, is an essential part of being God's child. As Paul wrote:

> Therefore, brothers and sisters, we have an obligation—but it is
> not to the flesh [that is, our inherited sinful tendencies], to live
> according to it. For if you live according to the flesh, you will die;
> but if by the Spirit you put to death the misdeeds of the body, you
> will live. For those who are led by the Spirit of God are the children
> of God. (Romans 8:12-14)

God Gives Me Wisdom to Make My Own Decisions

God the Father not only listens to his children when they pray—he also
speaks to them and guides them. An early church leader, James, makes this
promise: "If any of you lacks wisdom, you should ask God, who gives gen-
erously to all without finding fault, and it will be given to you" (James 1:5).

The clearest way that God gives his people wisdom is through his
Word, the Bible. In his letter to a young church leader, Timothy, Paul writes
this:

> But as for you, continue in what you have learned and have become
> convinced of, because you know those from whom you learned it,
> and how from infancy you have known the Holy Scriptures, which
> are able to make you wise for salvation through faith in Christ
> Jesus. All Scripture is God-breathed and is useful for teaching,
> rebuking, correcting and training in righteousness, so that the
> servant of God may be thoroughly equipped for every good work.
> (2 Timothy 3:14-17)

The Bible's primary task is to make us "wise for salvation" by telling us about
Jesus. Interestingly, Timothy's mother and grandmother were the ones who
first read the Bible with him when he was just a child. But in these verses we
see that by reading the Bible, we can also be "thoroughly equipped for every
good work." And that includes parenting!

I came across a reassuring story about some clueless parents in the
Old Testament. A "man of God" had recently prophesied to a lady that she
would conceive a son who would go on to save God's people from their
enemies. She reported this to her husband, Manoah, "Then Manoah prayed
to the Lord: 'Pardon your servant, Lord. I beg you to let the man of God
you sent to us come again to teach us how to bring up the boy who is to be
born'" (Judges 13:8)!

The Bible encourages us to do the same—to ask God for wisdom in
our parenting. I remember clearly the first time that I sat down in tears and

begged God for wisdom as a mother. Our eldest son was nearly three, and our days were full of temper tantrums. When I called out to God in the midst of my confusion, I felt strongly compelled to open up the Bible. And as I read, I felt for the first time that God was truly guiding me through my parenting dilemmas by giving me a new, godly perspective.

Although we might wish it were so, the Bible does not give us specific instructions for every parenting situation we will encounter. Instead, God teaches us clearly about the things that are most important to him; then he leaves us to apply these principles to our own life, with the wisdom he provides.

In a similar way, we cannot possibly prepare our children for every specific situation they will encounter. But we can help them to develop the wisdom to make their own decisions, based on the values we impart to them. In chapter 6, we will look in more detail at the different ways we can do this.

God Values My Long-Term Good above My Short-Term Comfort

In the Bible, love means seeking the good of another person. But from God's perspective, our long-term good does not always mean our short-term comfort. The following passage is from a letter written to Christians who were tempted to give up their faith in the face of hardship. Notice how God's loving parenting of his spiritual children sometimes involves unpleasant experiences for them.

> And have you completely forgotten this word of encouragement that addresses you as a father addresses his son? It says,
>
> "My son, do not make light of the Lord's discipline,
>
> and do not lose heart when he rebukes you,
>
> because the Lord disciplines the one he loves,
>
> and he chastens everyone he accepts as his son."
>
> Endure hardship as discipline; God is treating you as his children. For what children are not disciplined by their father? If you are not disciplined—and everyone undergoes discipline—then you are not legitimate, not true sons and daughters at all. Moreover, we have all had human fathers who disciplined us and we respected them for it. How much more should we submit to the Father of spirits and live! They disciplined us for a little while as they thought best;

Honor your father and your mother, so that you may live long in the land the Lord your God is giving you.

You shall not murder.

You shall not commit adultery.

You shall not steal.

You shall not give false testimony against your neighbor.

You shall not covet your neighbor's house. You shall not covet your neighbor's wife, or his male or female servant, his ox or donkey, or anything that belongs to your neighbor. (Exodus 20:2-17)

I used to think of the Ten Commandments as a list of "thou shalt nots." But beneath the prohibitions, they reveal the things that God wants his people to value most:

1. God wants his people to worship him—the one true God—only.

2. God wants his people to worship him, not the things he has created.

3. God wants his people to honor his "name" or character, as he has revealed it.

4. God wants his people to value both work and rest, tasks and relationships.

5. God wants children to respect their parents.

6. God wants his people to respect other people's right to life.

7. God wants his people to be faithful in marriage.

8. God wants his people to value other people's property.

9. God wants his people to value truth.

10. God wants his people to be content with what they have.

We can get so caught up in the tiny details of parenting techniques that we forget this overarching vision for Christian families. Let's take a closer look at some of the values reflected in these ancient commandments which have particular relevance for modern parents.

More Than Just "Family Values"

I found it surprising that "family values"—being a faithful spouse and a good parent—are not actually at the top of God's list of priorities. Rather, the first four commandments are about our relationship with God. God wants us to honor him above everything, including our family. According to the Bible, you cannot separate Christian values from the God who gave them.

Two Old Testament fathers illustrate this principle. One father, Abraham, was commended for putting obedience to God even above the life of his own son (Genesis 22); but the actions of another father, Eli, prompted God to ask, "Why do you honor your sons more than me?" (1 Samuel 2:29).

In the verses above, God calls himself a "jealous God." That may sound unreasonable at first, but there are certain contexts where jealousy is quite appropriate. One such context is in a marriage. If my husband did not keep his love and commitment for me alone, I would have a right to be jealous (and vice versa). In the Old Testament, God describes himself as a faithful husband to his people, and so rightly wanting their exclusive love and commitment. If people did not love God wholeheartedly, it was equal to "hating" him (in the words of the second commandment above).

Recently, we noticed that our neighbors' house was up for sale. We were surprised because they had only just finished landscaping the garden. I had seen the husband and a friend working hard to finish the deck, then watched as the two of them, looking sunburnt and satisfied, had "christened" it with a quiet beer. We thought the time had finally come for our neighbors and their young daughters to enjoy their new garden. But then the "For Sale" signs appeared. When my husband asked why they were selling, our neighbor explained sadly that he and his wife were "going their separate ways."

While they waited for the house to sell, the couple and their children were still living in the house together. I cannot imagine what it would be like to wake up each morning to face a spouse who no longer wanted to stay with me "'til death do us part." We wondered: Did they still cook meals for each other? Did they still wash up each other's plates? Or maybe they just shuffled around the house, trying to avoid each other. A marriage requires both people to commit wholeheartedly to each other, holding nothing back. If your spouse has decided they do not want to be married to you anymore, I cannot imagine that cooking you a meal or washing up your plate really means much.

A friend of ours has come up with some creative solutions to the problem of children receiving too many gifts at Christmas. She asks friends and relatives to give her children an "experience" as a gift, rather than a toy. For example, they might give the children a voucher to go to the zoo, or invite the children over to do some craft or cooking together. These experiences enrich the children's lives and relationships, without leaving them with an overabundance of toys. When it comes to buying gifts herself, she has taught her children to expect simply "something they want, something they need, something to wear, and something to read." These are some good ideas for helping our children practice contentment.

The challenge of the tenth commandment—not to covet or envy what our neighbours have—is particularly relevant to us modern parents and our children.

We have just seen how the Ten Commandments reveal some of God's Big Values, some of which are particularly counter-cultural. The fifth and seventh commandments, which concern marriage and parent-child relationships, are also very relevant, since they set out God's ideal structure for families. We will discuss these in detail in chapter 7.

Now, let's turn to another well-known part of the Bible which elaborates on the values behind the Ten Commandments: Jesus' Sermon on the Mount.

The Sermon on the Mount

By the time of Jesus' ministry on earth, many of God's people had fallen into the trap of thinking that simply keeping the "thou shalt nots" of God's commandments was enough. But in Jesus' famous Sermon on the Mount (recorded in Matthew 5-7), he reminds people of the values which lie at the heart of God's commandments. Let's explore how, in this sermon, Jesus shows that obedience to the Ten Commandments begins with a heart that values what God does—a heart that loves God and loves others.

The Heart of "Do Not Murder": Valuing Grace

Let's begin with the commandment, "Do not murder." In the Sermon on the Mount, Jesus claims that murder actually begins with the anger and hostility we allow to creep into our relationships with others:

> You have heard that it was said to the people long ago, "You shall not murder, and anyone who murders will be subject to judgment." But I tell you that anyone who is angry with a brother or sister will be subject to judgment. Again, anyone who says to a brother or sister, "Raca," is answerable to the court. And anyone who says, "You fool!" will be in danger of the fire of hell.
>
> Therefore, if you are offering your gift at the altar and there remember that your brother or sister has something against you, leave your gift there in front of the altar. First go and be reconciled to them; then come and offer your gift. (Matthew 5:21-24)

In saying this, Jesus taught that keeping the sixth commandment was about much more than simply avoiding the actual act of murder. It was really about being patient, kind, forgiving, and quick to reconcile with others.

Jesus went on to say that loving our neighbor means more than just being nice to our friends:

> You have heard that it was said, "Love your neighbor and hate your enemy." But I tell you, love your enemies and pray for those who persecute you, that you may be children of your Father in heaven. He causes his sun to rise on the evil and the good, and sends rain on the righteous and the unrighteous. If you love those who love you, what reward will you get? Are not even the tax collectors doing that? And if you greet only your own people, what are you doing more than others? Do not even pagans do that? Be perfect, therefore, as your heavenly Father is perfect. (Matthew 5:43-48)

We reflect the values of our Father by loving others as he does. And at the heart of God's love is grace—doing good to others, even when they do not deserve it. We do not love people only if they are loveable, but because God himself loves all people. This, then, is the Big Value behind the command, "Do not murder."

The Heart of "Do Not Commit Adultery": Valuing Marriage

Turning to the commandment, "Do not commit adultery", Jesus points to the fact that adultery actually begins with that first desirous glance towards another man or woman:

> You have heard that it was said, "You shall not commit adultery." But I tell you that anyone who looks at a woman lustfully has already committed adultery with her in his heart. (Matthew 5:27-28)

6

Passing On Our Values:
Practicing What We Preach

IN A RECENT STUDY in the USA called *The Children We Mean to Raise*, 80 per cent of the young people surveyed reported that they valued their personal achievement or happiness more than showing concern for others.[1] This came as a complete shock to their parents, who believed the opposite. It is one thing to establish clear family values, but quite another to successfully pass them onto our children.

Psychologist Leonard Sax believes that in the West, we are witnessing a breakdown in the process of "enculturation": social changes have significantly weakened family relationships, to the point where many children no longer learn their values from their parents, but from their peers and the media.[2] This calls for careful reflection about how we can pass our values on to our children.

In Part 2, we acknowledged the Big Problem of our human limitations—we are not perfect and we are not ultimately in control of who our children will become. Nevertheless, our children rely on us to guide them towards physical and moral maturity in line with our values. In this chapter I will share some basic principles for passing down our values to our children.

---

1. Weissbourd et al., "Children We Mean to Raise," 1.
2. Sax, *Collapse of Parenting*, chapter 1, section 2, para. 6.

The Foundation: Love and Understanding

In chapter 4, we saw that God's relationship with his spiritual children is founded on love: God accepts us as we are, provides for us, and listens to us. In the words of John, "See what great love the Father has lavished on us, that we should be called children of God! And that is what we are!" (1 John 3:1a) Knowing that we are dearly loved children of God is our motivation for living out his Big Values in the world—we want to make our Father proud.

It is similar for human parents—our children will only want to share our values if they know that that we will always love them. This means that our children should be able to count on our forgiveness when they do the wrong thing.

Unconditional love does not mean ignoring or excusing our children's bad behavior. In fact, it is *because* we love them that we do not overlook their behavior—we love our children so much that we want to see them mature. Ross Campbell's classic book, *How to Really Love Your Child*, gives some practical advice for how to show love to our children through eye contact, physical touch, focused attention, and loving discipline.

A strong relationship also depends on knowing our children, just as God knows us. We should work hard to understand each child—their personality, their interests, their worries, their strengths and weaknesses— the things that make them unique. But good parenting also requires us to understand our child's stage of development—the things that make them normal. This helps us to have realistic expectations, knowing the difference between bad behavior and simply childish behavior. A good parenting book can equip us with this knowledge (see my Recommended Reading list). For children with a disability, it will probably take more time and professional help to get to know their special needs and abilities.

The Most Precious Gift

Building a strong relationship with our children and passing on our values requires the one resource that modern parents seem to have in short supply: time. The best way to communicate love to our children is by spending focused, unhurried time with them. Getting to know them also happens most naturally by sharing meals, conversations, and activities. Psychologist Steve Biddulph has a good suggestion for balancing our time between our

> In the future, when your son asks you, "What is the meaning of the stipulations, decrees and laws the Lord our God has commanded you?" tell him: "We were slaves of Pharaoh in Egypt, but the Lord brought us out of Egypt with a mighty hand. Before our eyes the Lord sent signs and wonders—great and terrible—on Egypt and Pharaoh and his whole household. But he brought us out from there to bring us in and give us the land he promised on oath to our ancestors. The Lord commanded us to obey all these decrees and to fear the Lord our God, so that we might always prosper and be kept alive, as is the case today." (Deuteronomy 6:20-24)

The Israelites obeyed God's commandments because they were his rescued, chosen people. The New Testament echoes this sentiment:

> As obedient children, do not conform to the evil desires you had when you lived in ignorance. But just as he who called you is holy, so be holy in all you do; for it is written: "Be holy, because I am holy" . . .
>
> Now that you have purified yourselves by obeying the truth so that you have sincere love for each other, love one another deeply, from the heart. For you have been born again, not of perishable seed, but of imperishable, through the living and enduring word of God. (1 Peter 1:14-15, 22)

We love because we have become children of the God who loves. As parents we have a responsibility to teach our children our values with reference to the God who gave them. A simple way to do this is by regularly reading the Bible together (for some good Bible stories, retold for children, I recommend the *Jesus Storybook Bible* by Sally Lloyd-Jones or the *Big Picture Story Bible* by David Helm).

The phrase, "In the future, when your children ask you . . . ", occurs several times in the Old Testament (See Exodus 12:24-27, 13:14-16, Joshua 4:6-7, 21-24). Children were included in the Israelite community of faith from birth, but gradually came to understand and identify with their parents' values over time. An important part of this process was for parents to teach them and answer their questions.

As Western society drifts further away from the Christian values of the Bible, we will find that the values we seek to teach increasingly go against the prevailing culture of our times. Therefore, intentionally teaching our children about God and his values will take thought, time, and effort. But as we persevere, we will witness our children gradually filling in their picture of the world, and their place and purpose within it, based on what we teach.

Train Our Children

In most areas of modern life, we expect instant results; but the Bible reminds us that maturity only comes with practice. It describes the spiritually mature as those "who by constant use have trained themselves to distinguish good from evil" (Hebrews 5:14). As parents, we are not only role models and teachers, but trainers—helping our children to *practice* life skills and moral values.

Last year, our son's school announced that their class would be taking part in swimming lessons. Each week, they would catch a bus to a local pool where they would have the lesson, then change back into their school uniform and return to school. That night, our online parents' forum was abuzz with parent concerns: Would the children be able to dry and dress themselves? Would they remember to bring all their belongings home? One parent, who was also a teacher, shared her plan: she was going to practice those skills with her son every day until he could do them by himself. Simple! Our children will master the skills that we take the time to teach them.

I sometimes fall into the trap of seeing our children as obstacles to me doing my daily tasks—I look for ways to get them out of my hair. But after reading the Bible, I have come to see our children more as "apprentices" in need of training, rather than little consumers in need of entertaining. So I am gradually teaching them how to do simple chores like checking the mail, bringing in the garbage bins, sorting the washing, and setting the table. A few weekends ago, my husband managed to have hours of fun with our boys without spending a cent—they were washing the car together! Kids love spending time with us mastering a new skill, and feeling useful also boosts their self-confidence. Interestingly, every single parenting book I have read recommends that children do age-appropriate chores—they are an excellent way for our kids to practice doing things for others.

Daily life provides many other opportunities to train our children in doing good for others. A friend of ours is really good at this. For example, when my husband was recovering from a week in hospital last year, Rachael offered to come over with her daughters: she would help me with some cleaning while her daughters minded our children. Rachael's daughters are "apprentices" learning to doing good, not bored teenagers in need of entertainment.

Hand Over Responsibility

As parents, we have the goal of helping our children move towards physical and moral independence. This involves gradually letting them take more and more responsibility for themselves, according to their age and abilities.

The Apostle Paul talks about personal responsibility in this way:

> Carry each other's burdens, and in this way you will fulfill the law of Christ. If anyone thinks they are something when they are not, they deceive themselves. Each one should test their own actions. Then they can take pride in themselves alone, without comparing themselves to someone else, for each one should carry their own load. (Galatians 6:2-5)

We all need to take responsibility for our own "load"; but there are circumstances when a person's load becomes a "burden"—too much for one person to carry alone. Discerning the difference between a load and a burden is at the heart of parenting. If we carry our children's load for them, they will not learn to carry it themselves, and will lose the opportunity to develop a healthy sense of self-confidence. But if we do not help them when they truly need it, they will become discouraged. As our children grow and mature, we need to regularly reassess what is an appropriate load of responsibility for them to carry without our help. Parenting books and articles can help us do this (see my Recommended Reading list). However, no book can replace a deep awareness of each child's unique stage and abilities, which only comes from spending time with them.

Psychologist Judith Locke sees a growing generation of what she calls "bonsai children": children who have learnt to rely on their parents' help for things they really could do themselves. Locke has worked with university students whose parents still help with assignments, or give them a daily phone call to wake them up on time. As parents, we "overhelp" because we think it will help our children to achieve success and consequently high self-esteem. But in reality it has the opposite effect: children who have not learnt to do things by themselves begin to doubt their capabilities.[5]

Think of all the things we expect healthy adults to be able to do: get up on time, get washed and dressed, buy and prepare food, clean up after themselves, use public transport, work hard, budget their money, and so on. These are some of the basic life skills we are working towards as our children mature.

---

5. Locke, *Bonsai Child*, chapter 3, section 1, para. 6.

By the time our children are adults, they will be completely responsible not just for looking after themselves, but also for their own moral decisions. We can help them take responsibility for these decisions by not just laying down rules, but giving them the tools to decide for themselves what is right in a given situation. And then, once they have made a decision (whether good or bad), we can help them assess the result.

Here are some biblical questions we can use as tools to help our children make their own moral decisions:

- Would I want someone else to do that to me? (Matthew 7:12)

- Does that do good to others or harm? (Romans 12:21, Romans 13:10)

- Does that show respect for God? (Exodus 20:1-11)

- Does that show respect for my parents? (Exodus 20:12)

- Am I acting out of greed, anger, or pride? (1 Corinthians 13:4-7)

- Do the words I am speaking build others up or tear them down? (Ephesians 4:29)

- Am I taking good care of the things God has entrusted to me? (Matthew 25:23, Psalm 24:1)

- Am I reflecting God's values of generosity and grace? (1 Timothy 6:18, Ephesians 4:32)

As we progressively hand over more and more responsibility to our children for their own moral decision-making, we can expect them to grow in their understanding of our values, and the consequences of applying them (or failing to apply them); they will also grow in their ability to apply our values to new situations when we are not around.

Allow Natural Consequences

An important part of teaching our children to take responsibility for their choices is to refrain from stepping in to cushion them from the unpleasant consequences that sometimes follow.

The biblical book of Proverbs is written in the style of a father talking to his son about actions and their consequences. For example:

> Lazy hands make for poverty,
>> but diligent hands bring wealth.

Whoever walks in integrity walks securely,

    but whoever takes crooked paths will be found out.

Hatred stirs up conflict,

    but love covers over all wrongs. (Proverbs 10:4, 9, 12)

In a similar way, we can warn our children about the likely consequences of their choices. When it is safe, we can then allow them to experience these consequences for themselves. (For an example of when God himself did this to his people, have a look at 1 Samuel 8.) If we let our children experience the consequences of their decisions in small ways, they will learn to take responsibility for their actions, and make a habit of choosing the good.

When we say things like: "If you don't hurry up, you won't have time for television," "If you break your toy, we won't buy a new one," "If you don't do your homework, you will get in trouble at school," "If you feed your lunch to the ducks, you will be hungry," or "If you don't eat your dinner, you can't have dessert," we have to be prepared to allow our children to experience those consequences, no matter how unpleasant it will be for them (and us). The same is true in the world of values and morals. We need to teach our children that if they hurt other children or snatch toys, no-one will want to play with them. If they steal or tell lies, people won't trust them. If they don't honor God and other people, they will not experience the joy of living a life of purpose.

As our children get older, the stakes get higher. Some older friends have recently had to make the heartbreaking decision to tell their eighteen-year-old son to find somewhere else to stay. They had warned him repeatedly that if he did not respect them and the rules of their house, he could not live with them anymore. They had sought help and support for him, but when he refused to take it, they had to let him experience the consequence of his choices. Now they are waiting in hope for the day when he chooses to repent and come home to their love and forgiveness.

It can be hard to follow through with negative consequences because we have such a strong desire to protect our children from hurt and disappointment. However, it is vital to keep our sights on the bigger picture—we want to raise children who will take responsibility for themselves and their decisions when we are no longer around.

Beyond Consequences

God created us to live in a world where actions have predictable consequences. But the Bible is honest about the fact that sometimes, our actions do not have the consequences we expect. On the one hand, God himself sometimes steps in to cushion us from the consequences of our bad decisions—this is called grace. For example, on the cross, Jesus stepped in to experience the negative consequences of *our* sin so that we can be forgiven. Throughout our life, God can use even sinful actions and decisions to achieve something good in the long run. For example, the Bible tells the story of Joseph—a man who was betrayed by his brothers, sold as a slave, and then wrongfully imprisoned. Later on, Joseph was able to see how God had used his hardships for good. He forgave his brothers, saying, "You intended to harm me, but God intended it for good" (Genesis 50:20a).

On the other hand, good decisions sometimes have unpleasant consequences. Speaking the truth may disadvantage our career, being generous may leave us struggling financially, and being kind and patient can leave us vulnerable to exploitation. In some parts of the world, honoring God can even cost a person his or her life. The biblical book of Job is all about a man who lived a morally good life, but experienced great (yet unexplained) hardship. In the end, Job was forced to admit that God, our Creator, is free to rule the world however he chooses.

Teaching our children about consequences is important, but it is not the whole story. We were created to honor God and to love other people. This is the only path to a life well-lived and to eternal life with God, even if it sometimes takes us over rough terrain.

"Immunize" Our Children against Difficulty

As parents, we are responsible for preparing our children for life as adults in the real world, where difficult things sometimes happen. All of our parenting is built on the firm foundation of our unconditional love for our children. But on top of that (in fact, *because* of that), we need to "immunize" them against difficult experiences. By that I mean, we allow them to experience things like disappointment, sadness, failure, frustration, and boredom in small doses now, so that they will gradually develop the resilience they will need to overcome these potentially larger difficulties as adults.

7

Our Ideal Family Structure: Parents United and In Charge

IN CONTEMPORARY WESTERN SOCIETY, the nature of family life is in flux. In previous generations, most children grew up in a traditional family—raised by their biological, married parents, who exercised authority within the home. But for today's children, this situation is beginning to look more like the exception than the rule. Many people do not consider marriage to be a prerequisite for having children in the first place; and of the couples who do marry, around one in three will end up divorced (this is the current Australian figure; sadly, the rate is even higher in the USA and the UK).[1] New technologies also enable couples to become parents to children who are not biologically theirs. As a result of these changes, a growing number of children are raised by only one of their biological parents, either alone or with another partner. Modern families take many different forms.

Roles within the family are also being redefined. It is no longer taken for granted that a father will be the primary breadwinner or that a mother will stay at home to look after the children. The concept of authority has also fallen under suspicion, because of the way it has been abused in the past. There has been a movement away from the use of physical punishment to the point where giving your own child a smack (spanking) is illegal in twenty-four countries around the world. Because of these changes, many parents are reluctant to exert authority within the home; there is a new wave of parents who want to be friends with their children, and relate as almost equals. My own parents strongly believe that "Because I say so!" is a completely unacceptable response to a child.

1. McKenzie, "Marriages and Weddings", 1.

However, against the backdrop of human history, these changes to family life are incredibly recent. We are part of a huge social experiment, and the results are only just beginning to trickle in. Every human institution is made up of imperfect human beings, and the traditional family is no exception; likewise, there are many good and loving non-traditional families. But research continues to confirm that the traditional marriage is still the best option we've got—children thrive when their biological parents stay married and stay in charge.

All of this confirms the wisdom of what the Bible has been saying all along. God's ideal is for parents to share in the lifelong bond of marriage, and to exercise a loving authority over their children together.

Still Worth Striving For

Even though many modern families are broken, marriage is an institution too precious to give up on. The stability and commitment of marriage provides the ideal environment for children and their parents to flourish. In a healthy marriage, parents model how to forgive and do good to one another, no matter what; in a healthy marriage, parents model how to resolve conflicts with honesty and grace. Children who live with their biological, married parents, are also spared from the uncertainty and conflict that can sometimes arise when their parents bring new partners into their lives.

A large British study found that children who grew up in a traditional family were more likely to have better outcomes in health and education.[2] Australian national statistics indicate that living with your biological, married parents is a strong protective factor against abuse and mental health disorders.[3] These kind of findings have been replicated across the English-speaking world. In our modern world, a healthy, lifelong marriage is still an ideal worth striving for.

Living with Broken Dreams

Of course, only some families are non-traditional by choice. As I read through the Bible, I was surprised by how often God's people had to live with a family situation that was less than ideal. For example: Sarah's

2. Smallwood, "Focus on Families", 52, 67.
3. De Vaus, "Diversity and Change", 63-64.

husband, Abraham, slept with her maid in an effort to produce an heir; Joseph's brothers were so envious of him that they almost killed him; Naomi lost her husband and both sons within a decade; King David had an affair with a woman, got her pregnant, then had her husband killed; the prophet Hosea married a prostitute; and Mary had a baby out of wedlock.

However, these poor decisions or difficult circumstances became opportunities for God to demonstrate his grace and kindness. God forgave those who had sinned, and cared for those who had experienced loss—he was prepared to give them a fresh start. In fact, the children of broken families in the Bible often went on to do great things, in spite of their parents' mistakes and misfortunes. In Jesus' own family tree there were at least five children born to parents who were either unmarried or unfaithful, including King Solomon and Jesus himself (see Matthew 1:1-17).

Many of you may have a family situation that is not ideal; but God can redeem your difficult circumstances for his glory and for the good of your family. He can strengthen you to keep striving to raise children who honor God and love other people. If you are raising children on your own, it will be even more vital to have the support and encouragement of a wider family, whether biological or spiritual (this will be the topic of the next chapter).

If you are raising children who are not your own as an adoptive, foster, or step-parent, you can be part of God's plan to redeem an imperfect family. My husband's step-father has now been part of the family for twenty-one years. Even though my husband came from a broken family, the next generation—our children and their cousins—are benefiting from the example of my mother-in-law's second marriage to such a loving and faithful man.

Now let's have a look at what the Bible teaches about marriage and parenthood.

What Is Marriage For?

When I first read the Bible as a parent, it quickly became clear that it says a lot more about marriage than it does about parenting. In the Bible, the marriage relationship is the foundation of family life.

In Jesus' day, husbands had begun to find "any and every reason" to divorce their wives (Matthew 19:3). In those days, this left a woman without any way of providing for herself. In the face of this loose commitment to marriage, Jesus reaffirmed God's ideal:

> "Haven't you read," he replied, "that at the beginning the Creator 'made them male and female,' and said, 'For this reason a man will leave his father and mother and be united to his wife, and the two will become one flesh'? So they are no longer two, but one flesh. Therefore what God has joined together, let no one separate."
> (Matthew 19:4-6)

The biblical definition of marriage is when a man and a woman choose to make a break from their parents and make a public, lifelong commitment to one another. As they do this, God makes them "one"—they are no longer two separate individuals, but one new entity. Sex is a natural expression of this unity. Marriage is designed to provide the primary network of care and support for individuals—two adults take on the responsibility to care for one another and for any subsequent children "for better or worse." So with good reason, the Bible views faithfulness in marriage as the bedrock of society. The seventh commandment puts it simply: "You shall not commit adultery" (Exodus 20:14).

Of course, every marriage is made up of two imperfect people, who inevitably make mistakes and hurt one another. But the beauty of marriage is that those two people have promised to keep forgiving each other and to keep striving for the kind of love that puts the other first. The Bible says that this kind of marriage is a visual reminder of God's gracious love for his people (Ephesians 5:22-33, Malachi 2:13-15, Hosea 2:16-23).

In chapter 1, we saw that God made humanity—male and female—for the Big Purpose of honoring him and loving others. In marriage, as well as in other parts of our life, happiness is not our primary aim. Atheist philosopher Alain de Boton comments:

> [Modern marriage] has been rendered unnecessarily hellish by the astonishing secular supposition that it should be entered into principally for the sake of happiness . . . Christianity and Judaism present marriage not as a union inspired and governed by subjective enthusiasm but rather, and more modestly, as a mechanism by which individuals can assume an adult position in society and thence, with the help of a close friend, undertake to nurture and educate the next generation under divine guidance . . . Within the religious ideal, friction, disputes, and boredom are signs not of error, but of life proceeding according to plan."[4]

---

4. De Boton, *Religion for Atheists*, chapter 6, 5 para. 1-2.

I recently asked my grandmother about her view of marriage. She said that when she got married to my grandfather, there was only one thing she knew for certain: that it would be "forever." There was no way she could have known that now, sixty-five years later, she would be keeping her promise by faithfully visiting Grandpa in his dementia ward, even though he struggles to recognize who she is.

In recent decades, Western society has largely moved from this kind of covenantal view of marriage to a contractual one—marriage is now frequently seen as an agreement between two individuals, which can be dissolved if circumstances change. Today, many couples divorce because they no longer feel the same love they did at first. Modern marriage is more about feelings than promises.

However, making a marriage last takes more than feelings. In the words of Psychologist Steve Biddulph, "love starts as a blessing . . . but it continues as an achievement."[5] He claims that around 70 per cent of divorces could be avoided, if couples simply improved their communication and conflict resolution skills. Biddulph wisely comments, "The great majority of us marry people with hang-ups very similar to our own, and from whom we could learn a great deal if we were to persist."[6]

Similarly, the Bible teaches that marriage is not simply the expression of two people's momentary love for each other, but rather a couple's commitment to do good to one another, for better or worse, for the rest of their lives.

What If My Spouse Doesn't Share God's Values?

Both the Old and New Testaments strongly encourage God's people to marry someone who shares their beliefs and values, so that they can live them out without compromise (1 Corinthians 7:39, Deuteronomy 7:1-6).

However, the Bible also recognizes the reality that, for whatever reason, many people find themselves married to spouses who do not share God's Big Values. Sometimes, this ends up tearing the marriage apart. Paul speaks about that heartbreaking situation which was occurring in the early Christian church (he refers to Christians as "believers"):

5. Biddulph, *The Making of Love*, 17
6. Ibid., 18

If any brother has a wife who is not a believer and she is willing to live with him, he must not divorce her. And if a woman has a husband who is not a believer and he is willing to live with her, she must not divorce him. For the unbelieving husband has been sanctified through his wife, and the unbelieving wife has been sanctified through her believing husband. Otherwise your children would be unclean, but as it is, they are holy.

But if the unbeliever leaves, let it be so. The brother or the sister is not bound in such circumstances; God has called us to live in peace. How do you know, wife, whether you will save your husband? Or, how do you know, husband, whether you will save your wife? (1 Corinthians 7:12-16)

As far as it depends on us, we should work to keep our marriage together. Paul says that our unbelieving spouse and our children can still be "holy"; that is, they can still enjoy the blessings of being part of God's Family of believers, even if they have not personally become a child of God yet. Peter gives more advice on how to be a positive influence on a partner who is not a Christian in 1 Peter 3:1-7.

One of the early church leaders, Timothy, had parents with differing beliefs and values: Timothy's mother had come to believe in Jesus, but his father was a non-Christian Greek (see Acts 16:1-3 and 2 Timothy 1:5). In spite of this, Timothy's mother taught him the message of the Bible from a young age and he grew up to love God and serve his people as a church leader (2 Timothy 3:14).

Putting Your Marriage First

We have seen how much God values marriage as the foundation of family life. However, in the West, marriages are falling apart like never before. Experienced psychologist Andrew G. Marshall believes that many modern marriages are in trouble because husbands and wives have elevated their relationship with their children above their relationship with each other—they put their children at the center of the family, and take their spouse for granted. In these families, so much time, money, and energy is spent fulfilling the wishes of the children that at the end of the day, their parents don't have anything left for each other. Marshall has written a very helpful book, and the title says it all: *I Love You But You Always Put Me Last—How to Childproof Your Marriage*.

In the Bible, children are expected to honor their parents, primarily by listening to them. In Hebrew (the language of most of the Old Testament), the words "listen" and "obey" are the same—listening implies doing. But the reward of listening to our parents is priceless: their teaching is "the way to life" (Proverbs 6:23). Some parents expect their children to obey their commands immediately every time. However, Daniel and I take a more long-term view; we simply aim to cultivate a general pattern of obedience in our children over time.

It is right to insist that our children respect and obey us, because we are the ones who gave them life, we are older and wiser than they are, and we have their long-term good at heart. Coming to terms with this has gradually changed the way I speak to our children. I have slowly gained the confidence to give our children firm requests, rather than suggestions, and I have learned to make statements, rather than ask questions. For example, I now say, "Please put your shoes on; we are going to the shops" instead of "Why don't you put your shoes on? Would you like to go to the shops?" I have to regularly remind myself that, no matter what our children might think, we *do* (usually) know best!

Another important outworking of our parental authority is that we ought to make decisions on behalf of our children for the good of the whole family. Of course, we may give our children choices over smaller things (as long as we approve of all the options offered); but when it comes to significant decisions that affect the whole family, parents should make the final decision. By contrast, I have heard of parents who allow their children to have the final say on which school they will go to, where the family will go on holidays, or which house they should buy. Of course, parents will take the children's wishes into consideration, but the final decision should be up to them.

Children are called to honor both their father and their mother. So we should be careful to support, rather than undermine our spouse's authority in the eyes of the children. We should always speak respectfully about our spouse, and avoid correcting or contradicting them, especially when the children are around.

Clearly, honoring parents will look different, depending on a child's age. For young children, who cannot yet make moral decisions for themselves, honoring your parents means obeying them. For older children and teenagers, honoring your parents means showing them respect and appreciation, even if you have different opinions; when conflict arises, it means having a respectful discussion in order to reach a compromise. Adult children are still expected to treat their parents with respect, even if at times they have reason to disobey or disappoint them for the sake of their own values or conscience.

As our parents get older, the command to honor them implies caring for them as they age. Paul gave the following advice about the care of widows:

> Give proper recognition to those widows who are really in need. But if a widow has children or grandchildren, these should learn first of all to put their religion into practice by caring for their own family and so repaying their parents and grandparents, for this is pleasing to God . . . Anyone who does not provide for their relatives, and especially for their own household, has denied the faith and is worse than an unbeliever. (1 Timothy 5:3-4, 8)

It was a friend's mother, Mary, who first showed these verses to me. At the time, I was a university student with grand dreams of leaving everything behind to work with the poor overseas. But Mary's life showed me another side to serving God: these verses had inspired her to serve God by caring for her elderly mother. In her quiet, faithful way, Mary reflected God's love as much as any missionary.

In my own family, too, my parents and their siblings are faithfully caring for my grandparents in their old age. My aunt, Rosalind, and her husband purposely bought a new house which had a stand-alone cottage for my grandparents to live in. My generation now has a great example to follow when the time comes for us to care for *our* parents.

In God's ideal society, children honor their parents at every age.

Mothers and Fathers: What's the Difference?

The fifth commandment clearly says, "Honor your father and your mother"—both parents deserve equal respect. However, parents are not interchangeable. God created humanity as "male and female" (Genesis 1:27), not just two people exactly the same. Fathers and mothers are equal, but with different, complementary roles. To begin with, God created male and female such that only mothers can physically bear children. At the same time, the Bible also describes children as the "fruit" or "seed" of their father (Micah 6:7, Galatians 3:16). Parents are equally responsible for the creation of children, but in complementary ways.

As we have seen, the Bible affirms certain relationships of good and loving authority within society. In each of these relationships, there is no intrinsic superiority of one person over another—one is simply placed in a role of leadership. In line with this, the Bible teaches that husbands have been assigned the role of leader or "head" of their family, taking ultimate responsibility for the wellbeing of their wives and children. Ephesians 5:22-33 paints a beautiful picture of how a husband can lead by sacrificially serving his wife, for her good, and how a wife can respond by respectfully following his lead.

It might sound surprising, but when I read about a husband's ultimate responsibility, it brought me great relief. There is a common assumption that raising children is primarily the wife's job. In countless television advertisements, fathers are depicted as hopelessly irresponsible—as just another one of the children. If this were true, we mothers would carry a lonely burden. But the Bible makes a radical call to fathers to take responsibility for their children's physical and moral development, in partnership with their wives.

When Paul was describing the qualifications of a good church leader (literally, an "overseer"), he wrote:

> Now the overseer is to be above reproach, faithful to his wife, temperate, self-controlled, respectable, hospitable, able to teach, not given to drunkenness, not violent but gentle, not quarrelsome, not a lover of money. He must manage his own family well and see that his children obey him, and he must do so in a manner worthy of full respect. (If anyone does not know how to manage his own family, how can he take care of God's church?) (1 Timothy 3:2-5)

Paul expects that a husband will take the ultimate responsibility for managing his family, even though the day-to-day parenting is done by both parents. But notice the manner in which husbands are to exercise their responsibility: the ideal leader is self-controlled, hospitable, gentle, and not quarrelsome or greedy. Fathers are called to lead in line with God's values.

There is another passage which describes a father's unique role, also in a letter written by the Apostle Paul. He is speaking metaphorically about his leadership in terms of being a "father" (and a "mother"!) to the people he serves:

> Just as a nursing mother cares for her children, so we cared for you. Because we loved you so much, we were delighted to share with you not only the gospel of God but our lives as well. Surely

you remember, brothers and sisters, our toil and hardship; we worked night and day in order not to be a burden to anyone while we preached the gospel of God to you. You are witnesses, and so is God, of how holy, righteous and blameless we were among you who believed. For you know that we dealt with each of you as a father deals with his own children, encouraging, comforting and urging you to live lives worthy of God, who calls you into his kingdom and glory. (1 Thessalonians 2:7b-12)

The role of a father in Paul's mind seems to involve taking responsibility for his family by being a role model and by encouraging and urging his children to live out God's Big Values.

What I found really surprising was the picture the Bible paints of a mother's role in the family. I had made the mistake of assuming that the Bible promoted the ideal of the 1950s housewife: her domain was the home and she kept it to perfection. It is true that in Bible times, women did not usually have any paid employment outside the home. However, the activities of the ideal biblical mother certainly did not stop at home.

Take, for example, this poem about the "wife of noble character" in the Old Testament book of Proverbs:

> She gets up while it is still night;
>> she provides food for her family
>> and portions for her female servants.
> She considers a field and buys it;
>> out of her earnings she plants a vineyard.
> She sets about her work vigorously;
>> her arms are strong for her tasks.
> She sees that her trading is profitable,
>> and her lamp does not go out at night.
> In her hand she holds the distaff
>> and grasps the spindle with her fingers.
> She opens her arms to the poor
>> and extends her hands to the needy. (Proverbs 31:15-20)

The wife of Proverbs 31 is a provider, a property investor, and a businesswoman. She is industrious, yet generous both to those in her household and those outside. She spends time doing business and charity outside the home, but she also "watches over the affairs of her household" (Proverbs 31:27).

Similarly, the New Testament describes wives as the "managers" of the home, exercising leadership over children and any employees (1 Timothy 5:14). So the Bible seems to paint the picture of the husband as the spiritual "head" of the family, but the wife as the day-to-day "manager" of the home.

In the New Testament, we can gain some additional insight into the attributes of an ideal woman in the early church. In the following passage, Paul gives advice about which widows ought to qualify for practical support from the Christian community:

> No widow may be put on the list of widows unless she is over sixty, has been faithful to her husband, and is well known for her good deeds, such as bringing up children, showing hospitality, washing the feet of the Lord's people, helping those in trouble and devoting herself to all kinds of good deeds. (1 Timothy 5:9-10)

The "good deeds" expected of wives included not only being faithful to their husbands and bringing up their own children, but serving fellow believers and contributing to the needs of others in the wider community.

In our generation, women (including mothers) have unprecedented opportunities to join the workforce. Fierce debates now rage between those who work and those who do not—the infamous "mommy wars." The Bible does not make any particular pronouncements on this topic, but there are two key principles to remember. Firstly, God expects all his people, including women, to be involved in the community beyond their own family, expressing God's love by serving others (whether in a paid or unpaid capacity). We will look at this in more detail in the next chapter.

Secondly, as we have already seen, parents have the primary responsibility for raising their children to share their values—and this responsibility cannot be delegated. In the past, these two things probably happened at the same time—men and women simply took their children with them to "work" in the community. But today, most places of work outside the home assume that someone else will be caring for your children. Because of this, parents will have to seek creative solutions to balance contributing to the wider community and spending time raising their children.

Interestingly, the biggest cause of friction in modern marriages is the division of responsibility for child-rearing and housework.[11] In past genera-

11. Senior, *All Joy and No Fun*, chapter 2, section 2, para. 11.

tions, it was simpler—everyone expected that fathers would work full-time and mothers would stay at home. Neither of my grandmothers has had a paid job since they started having children over sixty years ago. By contrast, our generation is floating in "normlessness." For example, almost half of Australian mothers of primary-school-aged children work outside the home, mostly on a part-time basis.[12] But almost all women, even those who have demanding full-time jobs, continue to do the majority of the childcare and housework on top of their paid work.[13]

Women often have an expectation that the more paid work they do, the more their husbands will pick up the slack at home. But when these expectations remain unspoken, we end up falling into bad habits of resentment, nagging or "passive-aggressive" behavior. Andrew G. Marshall encourages women to clearly ask their husbands for the help they need, rather than just hoping they will offer or dropping cryptic hints.[14] Husbands and wives need to discuss their expectations in this area and come to an agreement that suits them both.

While the Bible seems to identify wives as the day-to-day "managers" of the home, many early Christian households had employees who helped with housework and even childcare, under the wife's leadership. So it does not seem to contradict God's ideal for families if women delegate "home duties" to other people, whether paid employees or perhaps their husband, to enable them to spend more time working outside the home. But once again, the ultimate responsibility for raising children who share our values lies with us, the parents. Whatever arrangement we come to will need to leave us with enough time and energy to nurture our family relationships.

In conclusion, then, a chorus of secular experts is now unconsciously falling into line behind biblical wisdom when it urges parents to build marriages that last and to be "authoritative"—warm, but firm—towards their children. The Bible places a high priority on the health of a marriage, for the sake of the entire family and community. Consequently, it encourages us to love our children enough to put them second—behind our spouse—and together with our spouse, to exercise a loving authority over them. Strengthening our family structure in line with God's ideals works out for

---

12. Crabb, *Wife Drought*, Introduction, para. 59.

13 Ibid., Introduction, para. 38.

14. Marshall, *I Love You But*, chapter 6.

the good of the whole family, providing a stable, safe environment where parents can lead and children can learn and grow.

8

God's Big Family: Belonging to a Wider Community

IT IS NO SECRET that many parents today are struggling to cope. There are many reasons why parenting in our era is hard, but one of them is that for the first time in history, we are trying to go it alone.

Our family situation is typical of our generation. My husband and I do not live in either of the communities where we grew up. Most of our friends also moved away to study, work, or buy a more affordable house. Even if we did live nearer to our parents, their houses would be empty during the week—all of them work full-time. The "stay-at-home grandmother" is fast becoming a vestige of a bygone era.

In the past, local neighborhoods provided strong networks of support for young families, including those who, like us, had moved from their childhood communities. Since most women were at home during the day, they knew each other and kept an eye on each other's children—raising children was a community affair. By contrast, our neighborhood is eerily quiet on weekdays. Another obstacle to us developing meaningful relationships with our neighbors is that we have moved house three times within a decade—a common feature of modern life.

So on a day-to-day basis, it is really just us. If I ever need help, it feels like the only person I can call on is my husband. Some weeks, he feels like he leaves one full-time job to come home to another. If one of the family is sick, or even if it is simply the school holidays, I can barely manage to keep the house running. I rarely ask my friends to help, since they are more or less in the same boat—"stuck" at home with little outside help. Most of them seem to manage doing a part-time job as well!

"Salvation belongs to our God,

who sits on the throne,

and to the Lamb." (Revelation 7:9-10)

Through Jesus, God is calling a new group of people to himself; but it is much bigger than one person, one family, or one nation.

God's New Family of Faith

Jesus completely redefined the word "family." According to Jesus, no longer is a person's family simply their blood relatives; children of God are also part of a spiritual family, which is made up of all those who believe in Jesus. The following incident illustrates this:

> While Jesus was still talking to the crowd, his mother and brothers stood outside, wanting to speak to him. Someone told him, "Your mother and brothers are standing outside, wanting to speak to you."
>
> He replied to him, "Who is my mother, and who are my brothers?" Pointing to his disciples, he said, "Here are my mother and my brothers. For whoever does the will of my Father in heaven is my brother and sister and mother." (Matthew 12:46-50)

This does not mean that Jesus neglected his earthly family. In fact, one of Jesus' final acts before he died was to provide a "son" (the apostle John) to care for his mother, who by that stage was a widow (John 19:25-27). Jesus also reaffirmed the two Commandments which dealt with family life: he called people to be faithful in marriage (Matthew 19:1-9) and to honor their parents (Mark 7:9-13). Jesus' life and teaching encouraged people to care for their natural family. But he also encouraged people to see themselves as part of the wider family of faith.

Now let's see how being part of God's Big Family of faith can shape our approach to parenthood today.

Parenthood in God's Big Family

Growing God's Family

We will now look at how the story of God's Big Family puts our human family into a new perspective. It changes the way we see parenthood, singleness, family conflict, and our children's place in the "family" of faith.

In the Old Testament, conceiving and giving birth to children was a vital expression of God's blessing. In the very beginning, God blessed Adam and Eve and commanded them to "be fruitful and multiply" (Genesis 1:28). God also promised to give Abraham many descendants as an expression of his blessing upon him. These descendants would become the nation of Israel, God's own chosen people—his children.

Jesus, however, taught that God's family would no longer grow through the natural birth rate, but would now grow by faith. In fact, Jesus—the only person who ever perfectly lived out God's purpose on earth—did so without ever marrying or having children. No longer was having biological children the primary way God intended to grow his blessed family.

Jesus also challenged the prevailing attitude that having children was the key to a blessed life:

> As Jesus was saying these things, a woman in the crowd called out, "Blessed is the mother who gave you birth and nursed you."
>
> He replied, "Blessed rather are those who hear the word of God and obey it." (Luke 11:27-28)

Jesus encouraged his disciples to focus not so much on getting married and having children (although many of them did that as a matter of course), but rather on growing God's family by telling people about God's offer of new birth through faith in Jesus. Before returning to heaven, the resurrected Jesus gave his disciples this commission:

> Go and make disciples of all nations, baptizing them in the name of the Father and of the Son and of the Holy Spirit, and teaching them to obey everything I have commanded you. And surely I am with you always, to the very end of the age." (Matthew 28:19-20)

Since the time of Jesus, the primary way God grows his Big Family is through people coming to faith in Jesus and being spiritually born again as children of God. People no longer become part of the "blessed" family of God by bloodline, but by faith.

husband received phone calls and messages of support from people of every rank. Several police visited him in hospital and brought him magazines to read—ones they had carefully chosen according to his interests. Once he was home, other colleagues brought around so many meals and groceries that our fridge was overflowing. Another colleague came and mowed the lawns for us and another offered to help with cleaning. Once my husband returned to work, he could not get much work done, because almost every person he saw wanted to stop and find out how he was doing!

This is the kind of "family" that God wants all his children to be a part of: a family where people know each other and are involved in each other's lives, enjoying the good times together and sharing the burden of the hard times.

This is how the historian Luke describes the early church family:

> They devoted themselves to the apostles' teaching and to fellowship, to the breaking of bread and to prayer. Everyone was filled with awe at the many wonders and signs performed by the apostles. All the believers were together and had everything in common. They sold property and possessions to give to anyone who had need. Every day they continued to meet together in the temple courts. They broke bread in their homes and ate together with glad and sincere hearts, praising God and enjoying the favor of all the people. And the Lord added to their number daily those who were being saved. (Acts 2:42-47)

When we are part of a wider family, we realize that as parents, we are not alone. In our modern society, where we are often distanced from our natural families, this is a very meaningful part of Christian family life. Christians of all ages can join together in helping to raise children who live out their Big Purpose in life. Our children can join in honoring God through worshipping him and doing good for others. And in turn, a supportive local church can provide the kind of practical support and encouragement that modern parents and children desperately need.

The call to join a wider family of faith challenges the modern mentality that each nuclear family is its own private entity that stands in competition with other families. Too often parents seem to be competing in their quest to be the perfect family. Some parents are caught up in an arms race, competing for the dubious honor of having the children who are proficient in the most number of skills. Other parents are masters at subtly fishing for information about other children's academic achievements, so that they can compare. Mothers seem to be competing for the title of "Supermom"—the one who has everything under control at home, excels in her chosen profession, looks effortlessly fit and glamorous, and still talks about her husband with a sparkle in her eye.

At a time when many parents feel confused and unsupported, we should be seeking to collaborate rather than compete with other parents. If we are confident in our purpose, our limitations, and our own values, then what other families are doing is no threat to us. The Big Purpose of our life on earth is to honor God and do good to others, which we cannot do if we are envying and competing with them. If we refuse to compete with other parents, but genuinely seek their good, the next generation will surely reap the rewards of growing up in a kinder and more supportive community.

When Our Two Families Are in Conflict

Children of God belong to two families—their spiritual family and their earthly one. So how do we balance our loyalty to these two communities of belonging? What should we do if our natural family does not belong to our wider family of faith?

Ideally, our biological family will simply be part of our spiritual family. But Jesus warned that sometimes, our own families may refuse to accept Jesus. In that case, there will be a conflict of interest. He said:

> Do not suppose that I have come to bring peace to the earth. I did not come to bring peace, but a sword. For I have come to turn
> "a man against his father,
>   a daughter against her mother,
>   a daughter-in-law against her mother-in-law—
>   a man's enemies will be the members of his own household."
> Anyone who loves their father or mother more than me is not worthy of me; anyone who loves their son or daughter more than me is not worthy of me. Whoever does not take up their cross and follow me is not worthy of me. Whoever finds their life will lose it, and whoever loses their life for my sake will find it. (Matthew 10:34-39)

If we seek approval from our family more than from Jesus, we are not worthy followers. If we want to "save" our life in an eternal sense, we have to "lose" our earthly, physical life—we need to hand everything we have over

CONCLUSION

Becoming Big Picture Parents

Eight Steps to Becoming Big Picture Parents

I BEGAN THIS PROJECT because I was overwhelmed by feelings of guilt, fear, and confusion as a parent. But as I read through the Bible of my ancestors, it lifted my gaze from the day-to-day dilemmas and decisions I was facing to see the bigger picture. The Bible teaches us about our Big Purpose as humans and parents; it shows us how we can cope with our Big Problem—our human limitations—by turning to God, the perfect Father; it teaches us the Big Values that we aim to pass on to our children; and it shows us God's pattern for families, within his Big Family of faith.

In this final chapter, I will distill what we've learnt from the Bible into eight steps we can all take in order to become the Big Picture Parents we were made to be.

Step 1: Discover Your Big Purpose

In chapter 1, we saw that God created humanity, both male and female, in his image: we were created for relationship with our Creator, his creation, and with each other. We were made like this for a Big Purpose—to honor God and love other people, by giving of ourselves for their good. God blessed humanity with the gift of marriage and sex, which produces a whole new generation of people who are created in God's image and inherit the same life purpose.

The first step to becoming a Big Picture Parent is to remember that happiness is not the primary aim of life for us or our children, but a by-product of living out our Big Purpose: honoring God and loving other people.

Step 2: Discover the True Purpose of Parenthood

In chapter 2, we saw that children share our human purpose, even from the womb. The purpose of parenthood is not only to conceive and give birth to children, but to protect their life, teach them, and guide them towards being able to choose the right and reject the wrong. In this way, we help our children to live out their God-given purpose.

The second step to becoming a Big Picture Parent is to see our children as people on the path to adulthood. We need to consider how we can help them grow towards physical and moral maturity.

Step 3: Accept the Big Problem of Your Human Limitations

In chapter 3, we recognized that we and our children have a Big Problem: we are born into an imperfect world. We fail to honor God and love others. We are powerless to keep our children safe in a world marred by sin and death. As parents, we will make mistakes that have a negative effect on our children. Our children's choices and experiences will disappoint us.

So the third step to becoming a Big Picture Parent is to accept our limitations. We need to aim not for perfection, but simply to be a "good enough" parent. We need to say sorry when we make mistakes and keep trying our best.

Similarly, we need to help our children cope with life in an imperfect world. We can help them to be patient and to persevere when things are tough. We can teach them to simply do their best, to say sorry when they get it wrong, and to keep trying.

Step 4: Find Freedom from Guilt and Fear in God's Perfect Fatherhood

In chapter 4, we saw that parenting in our imperfect world can lead to feelings of guilt and fear. But God invites us to stop trying to "have it all

> They will neither harm nor destroy
>> on all my holy mountain. (Isaiah 65:17-25)

In this world, we have to face the sad and frightening reality that our children are vulnerable to sickness and death. But in God's new creation, there will be no more crying. God will bless his people "and their descendants with them." This new creation—often called heaven—is the kind of place we will want to share with our children.

The Bible indicates that in heaven, our earthly family relationships will be subsumed by our relationship with God, our Father. Jesus said:

> The people of this age marry and are given in marriage. But those who are considered worthy of taking part in the age to come and in the resurrection from the dead will neither marry nor be given in marriage, and they can no longer die; for they are like the angels. They are God's children, since they are children of the resurrection. (Luke 20:34-6)

Heaven is for God's Big Family—his children—who have humbled themselves and trusted in Jesus' death for their forgiveness. In fact, Isaiah goes on to describe the experience of heaven (the "new Jerusalem") like being a baby receiving comfort from its mother:

> Rejoice with Jerusalem and be glad for her,
>> all you who love her;
> rejoice greatly with her,
>> all you who mourn over her.
> For you will feed and be satisfied
>> at her comforting breasts;
> you will drink deeply
>> and delight in her overflowing abundance.
> For this is what the Lord says:
> "I will extend peace to her like a river,
>> and the wealth of nations like a flooding stream;
> you will feed and be carried on her arm
>> and dandled on her knees.
> As a mother comforts her child,
>> so will I comfort you;
>> and you will be comforted over Jerusalem." (Isaiah 66:10-13)

Surely the greatest joy we could experience as parents would be to share heaven with our own children, because we have encouraged them to become not just our children, but children of God! Parenting on this side of heaven can be hard; but I pray that we will never lose sight of God's beautiful Big Picture.

APPENDIX

Questions for Group Study

Beginning Your Group Study

1. How do you feel as you begin to read *Big Picture Parents*? What are you hoping to gain from it?

2. In the Introduction, the author spoke about her own feelings of guilt, fear, and confusion as a parent. Can you relate to these feelings?

Note: All of the Bible verses mentioned in these studies can be found in the corresponding chapter of Big Picture Parents.

1. The Purpose of Life: Seeking More Than Happiness.

Introduction

1. What do you think your friends and family believe about the purpose or goal of life?

2. How do you normally react when your children are unhappy?

Take a few minutes to refresh your memory by looking over chapter 1 of Big Picture Parents.

Exploration

3. What do we learn about our human nature and purpose from Genesis 1:26-28?

4. How did Jesus summarize God's expectations of us in Matthew 22:37-39?

Application

5. Humans were created to rule over and enjoy God's creation. In which ways does your family interact with nature? How would you and your children benefit from connecting more often with this aspect of our humanity? How could you do this?

6. How can parents and children honor God, our Maker?

7. What does it look like in practice for us to "love our neighbor as we love ourselves"? What stops us from doing these things?

Discussion

8. In the Western world, there is a strong pressure to seek happiness through material possessions and comforts; modern families tend to have fewer children, but more "stuff". How does the Bible's teaching about our purpose challenge our aspirations?

2. The Purpose of Parenthood: Aiming for More Than Bedtime

Introduction

1. Have you ever felt a lack of purpose in your life or parenting? Have you ever felt like you were simply aiming to "survive" until bedtime?

2. How is your love for your children different from your love for other people, such as your siblings or friends?

   Take a few minutes to refresh your memory by looking over chapter 2 of Big Picture Parents.

Exploration

3. What does Deuteronomy 6:4-7 tell us about our role as parents?

4. If children are those who "do not yet know good from bad" (Deuteronomy 1:39), what does that mean for parents?

Application

5. In what ways do people in our society fail to protect children? Why do you think it happens?

6. How can parents take more responsibility for their children's moral development?

7. What are the "hot" parenting topics among your friends at the moment?

Discussion

8. Do you think that twelve/thirteen is a significant age of moral responsibility?

3. The Limits of Being Human: Our Guilt and Fear

Introduction

1. Do you ever feel like a bad parent? When?

   Take a few minutes to refresh your memory by looking over chapter 3 of Big Picture Parents.

Exploration

2. Read Genesis 3:14-19. How did the fall of humanity affect our key relationships with God, the creation, and each other?

3. What does God's warning to Cain in Genesis 4:6-8 teach us about sin?

Application

4. In the West, many people expect to be perfect parents providing the perfect childhood for their perfect children. What effect might these expectations have on us and our children?

5. Do you ever worry about "scarring" your children? How can we have a healthy attitude to our parenting mistakes, whether real or perceived?

6. We live in an imperfect world, where we cannot always stop bad things from happening to our children. How can we find comfort in the face of this frightening reality?

Discussion

7. To what extent do you think parents can take the blame (or the credit) for how their children "turn out"?

4. Parents in Need of a Parent: Finding Forgiveness and Comfort

Introduction

1. Have you ever felt lost and helpless as a parent? When?

   Take a few minutes to refresh your memory by looking over chapter 4 of Big Picture Parents.

Exploration

2. Jesus taught that people cannot come to God unless they "change and become like little children" (Matthew 18:2-4). What do you think he meant?

3. What does Romans 5:8 say about God's love for his children? How do these truths shape our sense of identity or self-esteem?

4. How can we experience God's fatherly love day-to-day?

5. What does Romans 8:28-29 tell us about God's ultimate purposes for his children?

Application

6. How can we show our children unconditional love, while still maintaining clear expectations for their behavior?

7. What role does God's empowering Spirit play in our life and parenting? What role could God's Spirit play in our children's lives?

8. How does God give us wisdom for parenting? How can we help our children to grow in wisdom?

Discussion

9. How does God's perfect fatherhood compare or contrast with what you have experienced of human fathers?

5. Christian Values: Remembering What Is Important

Introduction

1. What do you think were the three most important values in the family you grew up in? What kind of people were your parents striving to be? What attitudes and behaviors did they disapprove of?

   Take a few minutes to refresh your memory by looking over chapter 5 of Big Picture Parents.

Exploration

2. Do you remember the first four commandments (Exodus 20:2-17)? How would you summarize them?

3. Paul wrote that "love is the fulfillment of the law" (Romans 13:8-10). What do you think he meant?

4. In what ways did Jesus amplify the meaning of the commandments, "Do not murder", "Do not commit adultery", "Do not steal or covet", and "Do not lie" in his Sermon on the Mount?

Application

5. Which of the values behind the Ten Commandments and the Sermon on the Mount do you think are the most challenging for modern families? What are some practical ways that you can "swim against the tide"?

6. Which three values would you most like your own family to be known for?

Discussion

7. Do you think that your values have changed over time? How do you normally respond if you fall short of your own values and ideals?

6. Passing On Our Values: Practicing What We Preach

Introduction

1. Have you ever had the feeling that your children's values are not the same as your own? Have you ever been completely shocked by their attitude or behavior?

   Take a few minutes to refresh your memory by looking over chapter 6 of Big Picture Parents.

Exploration

2. Jesus warned his hearers about hypocritical teachers, saying, "Do not do what they do, for they do not practice what they preach" (Matthew 23:2-4). Are you ever guilty of this as a parent? How?

3. Paul wrote, "Carry each other's burdens . . . [but] each one should carry their own load" (Galatians 6:2-5). How does this apply to our role as parents?

4. How can our boundaries be a "law that gives freedom" to our children (James 1:25)?

Application

5. How can we build a strong relationship with our children, based on love and understanding?

6. How can we "immunize" our children for life in an imperfect world?

7. Biblical discipline is about helping our children to be "disciples" or "apprentices" of our values. What are the various methods we can use to do this? How can discipline be a "comfort" to our children?

8. How can we make sure that the things our children watch and read, especially on television and the internet, reinforce the values we want to teach them?

Discussion

9. What (and who) do you think are the biggest influences on the attitudes and behaviors of young people today? Which influences are the most supportive of your values?

7. Our Ideal Family Structure: Parents United and In Charge

Introduction

1. What do you think the word "family" means in today's world?

2. Do you naturally lean towards "warmth" or "firmness" in your parenting?

   Take a few minutes to refresh your memory by looking over chapter 7 of Big Picture Parents.

Exploration

3. Jesus said about marriage, "What God has joined together, let no one separate" (Matthew 19:4-6). How can we keep striving for this ideal in a world where divorce is so common?

4. Paul wrote about marriages in which one spouse is a Christian and the other is not: "if the unbeliever leaves, let it be so. The brother or sister is not bound in such circumstances; God has called us to live

in peace" (1 Corinthians 7:12-16). Are there circumstances in which divorce is inevitable?

5. What does Ephesians 6:1-3 teach us about God's ideals for parents and children? Is it ever right for children to disobey their parents?

Application

6. What role do feelings play in a marriage? Does it matter if a couple no longer "feels" in love with each other?

7. If you are married, what practical steps can you take to strengthen your marriage, and parent as a united team? If you are raising children on your own, how can you develop a strong network of support to help you in the task of raising children who share your values?

8. What does the authority of parents look like in practice? When do you find it hardest to exercise a loving (and united) authority over your children?

Discussion

9. In which ways do you hope your children will honor you, now and into the future?

8. God's Big Family: Belonging to a Wider Community

Introduction

1. What kind of community (or neighborhood) does your family belong to? Who do you turn to for help when you need it?

   Take a few minutes to refresh your memory by looking over chapter 8 of Big Picture Parents.

Exploration

2. God promised Abraham: "all peoples on earth will be blessed through you" (Genesis 12:2-3). How has this ancient promise been fulfilled? (See also Galatians 3:6-9.)

3. How do Jesus' instructions to his disciples in Matthew 28:19-20 apply to us as parents?

4. Jesus said that "anyone who loves their son or daughter more than me is not worthy of me" (Matthew 10:34-39). What do you think he meant?

Application

5. How do your friends and family view singleness? What kinds of unique opportunities might single people have?

6. What are some practical ways that your family can embrace those who have no family of their own to support them?

7. The Bible emphasizes the importance of belonging to a local "family of believers" (Galatians 6:10). How can we and our children be involved in a church community? How might this benefit our children?

Discussion

8. How do you think modern parents could collaborate rather than compete with each other for the sake of the next generation?

Concluding Your Group Study

Take a few minutes to refresh your memory by looking over the Conclusion of Big Picture Parents.

1. Has reading *Big Picture Parents* given you a new perspective on your role as a parent? Which ideas have encouraged you the most? Which ideas have challenged you the most?

2. The book concludes with the Bible's vision of the "new creation." On that day, God will live with his children and "will wipe every tear from their eyes" (Revelation 21:1-4). How does this vision of the future shape your approach to parenthood today?

Bibliography

Ainley, John, et al. "The Mental Health of Children and Adolescents: Report on the Second Australian Child and Adolescent Survey of Mental Health and Wellbeing." Canberra: Australian Department of Health, 2015. https://health.gov.au/internet/main/publishing.nsf/Content/9DA8CA21306FE6EDCA257E2700016945/$File/child2.pdf.

Biddulph, Shaaron and Steve Biddulph. *The Making of Love: Staying in Love as a Couple . . . Even With Kids.* Sydney: Doubleday, 1999.

Biddulph, Steve. *The Secret of Happy Children: Why Children Behave the Way They Do—and What You Can Do to Help Them to Become Optimistic, Loving, Capable and Happy.* New York: Marlowe, 2002.

Campbell, Ross. *How to Really Love Your Child.* 2nd ed. Colorado Springs: David C. Cook, 2003.

Clarke, Greg. *The Great Bible Swindle . . . And What Can Be Done About It.* Sydney: Bible Society Australia, 2013.

Crabb, Annabel. *The Wife Drought: Why Women Need Wives, and Men Need Lives.* Sydney: Ebury, 2014.

De Boton, Alain. *Religion for Atheists: A Non-Believer's Guide to the Uses of Religion.* London: Hamish Hamilton, 2012. Kindle edition.

De Vaus, David. "Diversity and Change in Australian Families: Statistical Profiles." Melbourne: Australian Institute of Family Studies, 2004. https://aifs.gov.au/sites/default/files/publication-documents/DiversityAndChange.pdf

Devon, Natasha. "Britain's child mental health crisis is spiralling out of control." *The Telegraph* 29 April, 2016. http://www.telegraph.co.uk/women/life/natasha-devon-britains-child-mental-health-crisis-is-spiralling/

Druckerman, Pamela. *French Children Don't Throw Food: Parenting Secrets from Paris.* London: Doubleday, 2012.

Eckersley, Richard. *Well & Good: Morality, Meaning, and Happiness.* 2nd ed. Melbourne: Text, 2005.

Harris, Russ. *The Happiness Trap: Stop Struggling, Start Living.* Wollombi: Exisle, 2007.

Locke, Judith. *The Bonsai Child: Why Modern Parenting Limits Children's Potential and Practical Strategies to Turn It Around.* Kelvin Grove: Judith Locke, 2015. Kindle edition.

Louw, Richard. *Last Child in the Woods: Saving Our Children From Nature-Deficit Disorder*. Chapel Hill: Algonquin, 2005.

McKay, Hugh. *The Good Life: What Makes a Life Worth Living?* Sydney: Macmillan, 2013. Kindle edition.

Mckenzie, Ashley. "Marriages and Weddings in Australia". Bella Vista: McCrindle Research, 2015. http://www.mccrindle.com.au/blog/MarriagesinAustralia_Media Release_McCrindle.pdf

Mangalwadi, Vishal. *The Book That Made Your World: How the Bible Created the Soul of Western Civilisation*. Nashville: Thomas Nelson, 2011.

Marshall, Andrew G. *I Love You But You Always Put Me Last: How to Childproof Your Marriage*. London: Macmillan, 2013. Kindle edition.

Oates, Kim. *20 Tips for Parents: The Realistic Parent's Guide to Understanding and Shaping Your Child's Behaviour*. Sydney: Finch, 2014. Kindle edition.

Palmer, Sue. *Toxic Childhood: How The Modern World Is Damaging Our Children And What We Can Do About It*. London: Orion, 2015. Kindle edition.

Perou, Ruth, et al. "Mental Health Surveillance Among Children—United States, 2005-2011." Atlanta: Centers for Disease Control and Prevention, 2013. http://www.cdc.gov/mmwr/preview/mmwrhtml/su6202a1.htm?s_cid=su6202a1_w

Sax, Leonard. *The Collapse of Parenting: How We Hurt Our Kids When We Treat Them Like Grown-Ups*. New York: Basic, 2016. Kindle edition.

Senior, Jennifer. *All Joy and No Fun: The Paradox of Modern Parenthood*. New York: Ecco, 2014. Kindle edition.

Skenazy, Lenore. *Free Range Kids: Giving Our Children the Freedom We Had Without Going Nuts with Worry*. San Francisco: Jossey-Bass, 2009.

Smallwood, Steve and Ben Wilson. "Focus on Families: 2007 Edition." London: National Statistics, 2007. http://news.bbc.co.uk/2/shared/bsp/hi/pdfs/04_10_07_families.pdf

Stutzman, Paul and Serena B. Miller. *More Than Happy: The Wisdom of Amish Parenting*. New York: Howard Books, 2015.

Weale, Sally. "Child mental health crisis 'worse than suspected.'" *The Guardian* 29 April 2016. https://www.theguardian.com/society/2016/apr/29/government-expert-warns-child-mental-health-crisis-worse-than-suspected.

Weissbourd, Rick, et al. "The Children We Mean to Raise: The Real Messages Adults Are Sending About Values." Cambridge: Harvard Graduate School of Education, 2014. http://mcc.gse.harvard.edu/files/gse-mcc/files/mcc-research-report.pdf.

Lightning Source UK Ltd.
Milton Keynes UK
UKOW01f2109140717
305352UK00001B/35/P

9 781532 602535